PHILOSOPHY OF LANGUAGE

THE BASICS

This book provides beginners with a sense of the questions and methods that make up the philosophy of language. The first four chapters develop the idea that language is a system that allows us to exchange information with each other, and the second four chapters explore the idea that language is a tool we can use to perform actions, like promising, insulting, and socially positioning ourselves.

The first part of the book traces an arc connecting questions like:

- What is language?
- Where does meaning come from?
- How do we use meanings to send messages to each other?

The second part of the book takes up questions like:

- Does pornography silence women?
- What is offensive about slurs?
- What do we lose when languages go extinct?

With a glossary of key terms, questions for reflection, and suggestions for further reading, *Philosophy of Language: The Basics* is the place to start for anyone who is curious about how high the seas of language rise.

Ethan Nowak is Senior Lecturer in Philosophy at Cardiff University in Wales.

THE BASICS

The Basics is a highly successful series of accessible guidebooks that provide an overview of the fundamental principles of a subject area in a jargon-free and undaunting format.

Intended for students approaching a subject for the first time, the books both introduce the essentials of a subject and provide an ideal springboard for further study. With over 50 titles spanning subjects from Artificial Intelligence to Women's Studies, *The Basics* is an ideal starting point for students seeking to understand a subject area.

Each text comes with recommendations for further study and gradually introduces the complexities and nuances within a subject.

AMERICAN PHILOSOPHY
Nancy Stanlick

PHENOMENOLOGY
Dan Zahavi

ANIMAL ETHICS
Tony Milligan

ATHEISM
Graham Oppy

ARTIFICIAL INTELLIGENCE
Kevin Warwick

EMOTION
Michael Brady

EVOLUTION
Sherrie Lyons

PHILOSOPHY OF MIND
Amy Kind

PHILOSOPHY (fifth edition)
Nigel Warburton

METAPHYSICS (second edition)
Michael Rea

GLOBAL JUSTICE
Carl Death and Huw L. Williams

FREE WILL (second edition)
Meghan Griffith

HUMAN GENETICS (second edition)
Ricki Lewis

CRITICAL THINKING (second edition)
Stuart Hanscomb

LOGIC (second edition)
J.C. Beall

GLOBAL DEVELOPMENT
Daniel Hammett

BIOETHICS (second edition)
Alastair V. Campbell

FOOD ETHICS (second edition)
Ronald Sandler

EASTERN PHILOSOPHY (second edition)
Victoria Harrison

Other titles in the series can be found at:
https://www.routledge.com/The-Basics/book-series/B

PHILOSOPHY OF LANGUAGE

THE BASICS

Ethan Nowak

Routledge
Taylor & Francis Group

NEW YORK AND LONDON

Designed cover image: Getty Images

First published 2025
by Routledge
605 Third Avenue, New York, NY 10158

and by Routledge
4 Park Square, Milton Park, Abingdon, Oxon OX14 4RN

Routledge is an imprint of the Taylor & Francis Group, an informa business

© 2025 Ethan Nowak

The right of Ethan Nowak to be identified as author of this work has been asserted by them in accordance with sections 77 and 78 of the Copyright, Designs and Patents Act 1988.

British Library Cataloguing-in-Publication Data
A catalogue record for this book is available from the British Library

ISBN: 978-1-032-16877-7 (hbk)
ISBN: 978-1-032-16867-8 (pbk)
ISBN: 978-1-003-25075-3 (ebk)

DOI: 10.4324/9781003250753

Typeset in Bembo
by KnowledgeWorks Global Ltd.

CONTENTS

ACKNOWLEDGMENTS

Para mi ñaña Cecilia Vaca Jones

I feel very fortunate to have had the chance to learn from many excellent philosophers, linguists, and language teachers, and I hope that no one will blame them for the mistakes I will inevitably make here. I'd like to particularly thank Daniel Harris for very helpful discussion, Eliot Michaelson and an anonymous referee for detailed comments that greatly improved previous versions of this manuscript, and Stephen Laurence for the image that I reproduce with his permission on pg. 167 (Figure 7.1).

I will always be extremely grateful to my parents and to my partner for being so patient, loving, and supporting that I have gotten to spend as much time as I have thinking about words and what we do with them.

PREFACE

As the title suggests, the aim of this book is to provide the reader with an introduction to the basics of the philosophy of language. I have not tried to cover everything that could plausibly be considered part of the basics, or even tried to follow all of the twists and turns of each of the arguments I do present. Instead, I've tried to choose topics and a level of detail that I think will help newcomers to the field to see how the some of the major pieces fit together. My hope is that the structure I provide here, which is the structure I use when teaching the philosophy of language myself, will provide readers with a foundation that can be naturally extended to accommodate the many topics that didn't fit into this book.

After every chapter, I'll provide both the key references the chapter was based on – what I'd typically assign as reading if I were teaching that chapter – and some suggestions about further material that might be interesting. In many places, those suggestions will refer to the Stanford Encyclopedia of Philosophy (SEP). The SEP is an excellent resource that I often recommend to my students – if I myself were to suddenly develop an interest in a new area of philosophy, I'd start by reading the SEP article on that area, and then reading some of the papers cited there, some of the papers cited in those papers, and so on. Since the SEP editors and authors regularly update the content there, I expect it will reflect ongoing developments better than any other source I could mention here.

For readers interested in a synthesizing approach like the one I take here but pitched a level up, William Lycan's Routledge textbook *Philosophy of Language: A Contemporary Introduction* is rightly regarded as a classic.

For readers who want the primary sources collected in one place, I recommend A.P. Martinich and David Sosa's Oxford anthology *The Philosophy of Language*.

Part I

INFORMATION EXCHANGE

WHAT IS A LANGUAGE?

1.1 FIRST STEPS TOWARD A DEFINITION

This book is an introduction to the philosophy of language. As the name suggests, the philosophy of language is the research field concerned with philosophical questions raised by language and language use. What kinds of questions are these? Among the topics that have been prominent in the philosophical literature, we find questions about what kinds of things linguistic meanings are and where they come from, questions about the relationship between the things a person thinks and the things they say, questions about the relationship between the things a person says and the way the world is, and much more. Throughout the book, we will explore these and other topics in detail, but a good strategy for working our way into those questions is to start with some that are a bit more general: what do people who share a language share? What do people who don't share a language lack? What even is a language in the first place?

At first glance, these might seem like somewhat strange or even silly questions. Nearly every human being who ever lived has known at least one language, and most of us have no trouble at all naming a handful or more, identifying them when we hear or see them, and so on. To say much beyond 'I know a language when I see one', however, turns out to be surprisingly difficult.[1]

DOI: 10.4324/9781003250753-1

1.1.1 LANGUAGE AS A SYSTEM FOR INFORMATION EXCHANGE

So, what is a language? Since we have to start somewhere, consider the following attempt at an answer:

> A language is a system that allows agents to exchange information.

Something about this seems right. Think about the last conversation you were involved in, or about what's been happening as you read these words. Whatever else we might be up to when we use language – having fun, trying to make each other laugh, feel cared for, etc. – typically when we sign, speak, write, or interpret someone doing these things, information is being exchanged. That seems like a point in favor of our definition. Another point may be added if we consider what happens when we meet people we don't share a language with: our ability to exchange information is the most obvious thing to suffer.

This first attempt at a definition of language seems to include too much, however. Think more about how we manage to get by in cases where we would normally say we don't share a language with someone. Suppose I know only English, and you know only Urdu. If I'm sitting in a market stall with a pile of apples and you want to buy two, you will probably be able to get that much across by pointing at the apples and holding up two fingers. Maybe you'll show me your wallet, or mime taking a bite out of your fist. This doesn't seem like a linguistic exchange, but information is certainly conveyed.

A gruesome biblical story that has featured in many prominent philosophical discussions of language can be used to make a similar point. In order to fulfill a promise to Salome, King Herod ordered his men to cut off the head of John the Baptist. When Salome eventually receives the head on a platter, she comes to learn that John is dead and that the promise has been fulfilled. As in our market case, information has clearly been exchanged here, although no one has had to utter a word (write, sign, etc.). Anyone present, whether they shared a language with the soldiers or with Herod or Salome or not, would themselves come to know that John was dead.

These examples show that we can exchange information without using language. At this point, you may be wondering 'Hmm, but how is that a problem for our definition? Didn't we say that language was supposed to be a *system* for exchanging information? Here there doesn't seem to be anything systematic going on … so do these examples really show that our definition was too inclusive?' If you are thinking along these lines, great – that is exactly the kind of reaction a philosopher would have! But there are good reasons to think that these examples *do* in fact illustrate a problem for our initial attempt to say what language is.

While Herod doesn't have to rely on any system when he shows Salome that John is dead, it is not hard to think of ways in which we could make showings of proof that promises have been kept systematic. In fact, you might think something like this actually happens in places where hunters are paid for killing members of certain problematic invasive species – upon presentation of an animal carcass, a bounty is paid. To take a class of less upsetting examples, consider systems that might evolve in a workplace, whereby one person leaves a stack of folders or widgets at a certain stage of production in a prominent place so that others will know when a task is complete. Or think of a system we might develop where we leave our office blinds open when we go out for lunch so that others can see we are not available to meet.

While systems like these clearly involve the exchange of information, it is just as clear that they do not involve language. Anyone who sees the pile of widgets on my empty desk, regardless of whether we share a language or not, will come to know that the widgets have been produced or that I am out. So merely adding a requirement of systematicity to our original definition doesn't narrow things down in quite the way we seem to require.

All that said, even if it turns out that not just any kind of systematicity will do, it does seem right to say that systematicity is an important feature of language. So what kind of systematicity makes a method of information exchange into a language? Think again about the examples we've just considered, of John the Baptist or the office blinds. One way to put the point these examples make would be to say that there is an important difference between providing someone with some information by *showing* them something – that is, between offering information by non-linguistic means – and providing them with some information by *telling* them something – that is, offering information by linguistic means.

1.1.2   LANGUAGE AS AN ARBITRARY SYSTEM

Ferdinand de Saussure, a Swiss academic working in the late 19th and early 20th century who is considered by many to be the first modern linguist, offered a take on this difference that many of today's philosophers of language continue to endorse in one form or another. For de Saussure, the key thing that distinguishes languages from other sorts of systems we might use to exchange information is the property of **arbitrariness**.

To see what arbitrariness amounts to in this context, let's start by looking at some **non-arbitrary** ways in which information might be encoded. Think again about the relationship between the severed head of John the Baptist and the information that John is dead. The reason the head is an effective indicator of John's death is precisely that it would not be possible to be confronted with it if he were still alive. Examples of less direct, but still non-arbitrary information-encoding relationships include things like tree rings and tracks in the snow; the rings of a tree form each year, so counting the rings will tell you its age, and tracks are the physical record of some animal's progress over the terrain.

Contrast the relationship between the words 'John the Baptist is dead' and the information that John is dead. Here the connection between the thing that conveys information – a sentence – and the information that is conveyed is much looser. Nothing about the sound or shape of the words themselves or the sentence they form seems to involve any intrinsic connection to the information they represent; the word 'dead' doesn't look or sound like death, whatever that would mean. While there may be a few words here and there that sound like the things they apply to – a quick search turned up 'sizzle', 'buzz', and 'hiss' as examples – these are exceptions that prove the rule. Most of the words that make up natural languages have no resemblance to the things they pick out, and where multiple languages use a similar word for a similar thing, we typically take this to be evidence of a historical connection between them, as opposed to some deep metaphysical connection between the word and whatever worldly phenomenon it is applied to.

Because it is so widely assumed, philosophical discussions tend not to explicitly emphasize this point about the arbitrariness of linguistic systems. Nevertheless, we can see the idea at work throughout standard contemporary philosophical thinking about language. Consider the following definition offered by one of the most influential 20th-century philosophers of language, David Lewis:

> What is a language? Something which assigns meanings to certain strings of types of sounds or of marks. It could therefore be a function, a set of ordered pairs of strings and meanings. The entities in the domain of the function are certain finite sequences of types of vocal sounds, or of types of inscribable marks; if σ is in the domain of a language $\mathcal{L}$, let us call σ a sentence of $\mathcal{L}$. The entities in the range of the function are meanings; if σ is a sentence of $\mathcal{L}$, let us call $\mathcal{L}(\sigma)$ the meaning of σ in $\mathcal{L}$.
> (Lewis 1975, 3)

While Lewis' definition might look intimidating, it is worth taking some time to unpack, as it will put us in a good position to set up a map of the kinds of discussions that have occupied philosophers of language in recent years. Also, while the terminology is sophisticated, the basic idea turns out to be fairly straightforward.

Let's start with the notion of a **function**. If you remember the idea from school, great, but if not, no problem. Functions are a kind of abstract object, which we usually describe in one of two ways. On the first way of thinking, we treat them as rules that take a certain input and yield a certain output. So, two functions are different only if there's some object that, when treated as input, returns a different output. And something that takes a single input and returns varying outputs isn't a function in our sense.

The most familiar examples of functions probably come from math – something that's usually called the 'successor function', for example, takes a natural number and yields the number that follows it in the number sequence (1, 2, 3…). Given 1 as input, the function returns 2 as output. Given 2 as input, it returns 3 as output, and so on. (You might see this expressed as the '+1' function.) Addition is a function, too – specifically, the function that takes a pair of numbers as inputs and returns their sum as output. The subtraction function takes a pair of numbers as inputs and returns their difference as output, and so on.

On the alternative way of thinking that Lewis mentions, we can describe a function by providing a set of pairs of objects, where the order of the members of the pair matters (so the two pairs that can be formed from just the numbers 1 and 2, which we write as $<1,2>$ and $<2,1>$ are not the same). Put this way, the successor function would be the set of pairs: $<1,2>,<2,3>,<3,4>,...$ and the addition function a set of pairs (whose first member is itself a pair): $<<1,2>,3>,<<2,3>,5>,....$

While mathematical examples are the most familiar, we can build functions from whatever kinds of objects we like. If we wanted to, we could use the rule-style formulation to define the function that takes the objects currently on my desk and returns the person who owns them. In ordered-pair terms, that would be the set of pairs: <Ethan's wallet, Ethan>, <Ethan's phone, Ethan>, <Ethan's dad's car keys, Ethan's dad>. Or we could define the function that takes an object from my desk and returns the number 1 if the object is mine, and 0 otherwise (think of this as a test for the property of being owned by me). In set terms, that'd be <Ethan's wallet, 1>, <Ethan's phone, 1>, <Ethan's dad's car keys, 0>.

PRACTICE: Can you describe a mathematical function using the rule formulation? Now do it using the formulation in terms of a set of ordered pairs. Can you describe a function mapping ordinary objects into 1,0 using the rule formulation? Using the set formulation?

Lewis doesn't care – and neither will we – about differences between these two ways of describing functions. What's important for him is the claim that we can use the notion of a function to say what language is. Instead of a function that takes one number and returns another number, Lewis thinks that languages are just functions that take a string of words or sounds – a sentence in the language – and return meanings. Or, in set terms, a language is a set of pairs of objects where the first member of each pair is some sentence from the language and the second member its meaning.

Before we take up the question of what a meaning is, we should pause to clarify one point about sentences. When Lewis talks about a function that maps sentences into their meanings, it is important to note that he is talking about sentence **types**, not individual utterances as they are produced on a particular occasion, which philosophers call sentence **tokens**.

To see the difference between types and tokens, consider a classic example. Suppose you have two copies of *Waverley* and one copy of the *Analects* on your desk and someone asks 'How many books are on your desk?' If you are counting book tokens, you should say: 'three – two copies of *Waverley* and one of the *Analects*'. But if you are counting book types you should say: 'two – *Waverley* and the *Analects*'. If someone asks 'How many letters are in the word 'waffle'?' you might respond with either '5' or '6', depending on whether you are talking about letter types or letter tokens (since there are 2 'w' tokens). With all of this in mind, we can identify a sense in which two people can utter the same sentence, and a sense in which they cannot. So, if Ashley and Bailey both say 'I wish this guy would stop talking about types and tokens already', we might say that they produce the same sentence type but not the same sentence token.

There are important philosophical questions that have been raised about when a particular series of sounds or signs that someone produces on an occasion should count as a token of a certain sentence type. Are the sentences 'Green is a color' and 'Green is a colour' tokens of the same sentence? How about the pronunciations of them as produced by a British person and an American? For now, however, we will set these issues aside and assume that different spellings and pronunciations like these count as realizations of the same sentence type. Crudely, we can use the criterion: if your middle-school teacher would have said two things are the same sentence, we will treat them as the same sentence.

So much for the input side of the language function, or the first position in the ordered pair. Taking up our main thread again, we can ask: what about the output side, or the second position in the pair? Here, things might seem a bit mysterious. It's easy enough to see what a function is when it involves numbers or ordinary objects. We can sort of squint and imagine how a function might take sentence types as its arguments – while types sound a bit abstract, we don't struggle to identify tokens, (sequences of sounds or marks on a page), so we can maybe imagine ways the type might be defined in terms of its tokens.

> Can you think of a way to define a sentence type in terms of sentence tokens?

But what kind of thing is a sentence meaning? This might sound, on the face of things, like a deeply puzzling philosophical question. When we look around the world, we see lots of what the philosopher J.L. Austin is often quoted as calling 'medium-sized dry goods': there are rocks and trees, furniture and cars, people and animals. We know that in some sense numbers are around, too, and maybe even properties like beauty or justice. Meanings, however, seem pretty clearly not to be the sort of thing you could stub your toe on, and not obviously something that lives in the same place numbers and properties do, either. This seems like a problem for our attempt to treat language as a kind of function.

Meanings are truth conditions

As it turns out, however, and as is so often the case in the discipline, philosophers have a way of dissipating the mystery. The passage we quoted earlier from Lewis continues like this:

> What could a meaning of a sentence be? Something which, when combined with factual information about the world – or factual information about any possible world – yields a truth-value. It could therefore be a function from worlds to truth-values – or more simply, a set of worlds.
> (Lewis 1975, 3)

We saw earlier how Lewis said that language is a function from sentences to meanings. Now he is saying that meanings themselves are functions from possible worlds into truth values? Although that might sound very confusing, here again we can make sense of the proposal if we walk through it slowly.

The idea that Lewis is giving expression to in this passage is one that many philosophers have endorsed in various forms; particularly prominent proponents include Gottlob Frege and Donald Davidson. In a nutshell, the idea is that the meaning of a sentence is a condition that it imposes on the world – in order for the sentence to be true, the world must be a certain way.

Different sentences, as you might guess, impose different conditions. So, in order for the sentence 'Antananarivo is the capital of Madagascar' to be true, Antananarivo has to be the capital of Madagascar (in fact, it is and the sentence is true). For the sentence 'the continuum hypothesis is undecidable' to be true, the world has to be a certain way – namely, the continuum hypothesis has to be undecidable (Wikipedia says it is, but I'm not in a position myself to say). And so on.

The idea that the meaning of a sentence is its truth conditions is one that we can provide quite solid intuitive support for. Think about what you know when you know the meaning of a sentence. Suppose, for example, that I tell you that my cat, Chaiya, is a mixed Siamese and domestic shorthair. Unless you know her, you won't know whether the sentence 'Chaiya is a mixed Siamese and domestic shorthair' is true or not. But if you know English, you know how the world *would have to be* in order to make the sentence true. You can sort of close your eyes and think of all the different scenarios that would be compatible with Chaiya being a mixed Siamese and domestic shorthair, and all the different scenarios that would be incompatible with that condition.

To approach the same intuition from a different angle, imagine someone who, anytime they heard a sentence of English, knew how the world had to be in order for the sentence to be true but claimed not to know English. If we set miracles or advanced technologies aside, it seems like it would be hard to take their claim very seriously – if the person's ability is sufficiently general, so that given any sentence of English (or nearly any), they can describe how things would have to be in order for the sentence to be true, it seems like we'd have to say they know English!

The same point can be made by considering someone in the opposite position, that is, someone who claimed to know English, but couldn't, given sentences of English, reliably say what their truth conditions are. What reason would we have to say that such a person knows English? We certainly would not expect them to do very well on English language exams![2]

The foregoing considerations are meant to warm you up to the idea that the meaning of a sentence is its truth conditions. But still, you might ask: what exactly are truth conditions? Lewis offers two equivalent answers to this question. He says we can treat truth conditions as functions from possible worlds to truth values, or as sets of possible worlds. By truth values, he just means true and false, which are sometimes represented in writing with the numbers 1 and 0.

Philosophers have different views about what possible worlds are, but we don't have to take a position on that question in order to use the idea. For our purposes it'll be enough to say a possible world is a way things could be – a set of answers to all the questions, a way of fixing all the facts, and so on. There is a possible world – in fact, many, many possible worlds – in which Hilary Clinton won the 2016 election. There are worlds in which she won and it snowed at the inauguration, worlds in which she won and it did not snow, and worlds in which she won and Trump apologized for leading chants of 'lock her up', worlds in which she won and he did not apologize. There are worlds in which you won the election, worlds in which I did, worlds in which the winner was your dog, and so on. Anything you can imagine is a way a world can be, and thus a way some possible worlds are.[3]

Think of a sign at a carnival that says: 'You must be 48 inches/120 centimeters tall to ride this ride'. That sign separates the human population into two groups, those who meet the condition and are thus allowed to ride, and those that do not and who thus must wait outside. Truth conditions do something very similar, except instead of separating people into groups they carve up the space of possible worlds.

We said earlier that the sentence 'Antananarivo is the capital of Madagascar' sets out a condition: Worlds where Antananarivo is the capital of Madagascar meet it, while worlds where some other city is the capital of Madagascar do not.[4] We can model the truth condition that sentence expresses, then, by using those two sets of worlds. We call the worlds in which Antananarivo is the capital of Madagascar **verifiers** of the sentence, the worlds in which it is not its **falsifiers**, and we say that the set of verifiers is the **proposition** the sentence expresses. Equivalently, we can say – with Lewis – that the proposition in question is a function that takes worlds from the set of verifiers and returns 1, and worlds from the set of falsifiers and returns 0.

1.2   NARROWING THINGS DOWN: NOT JUST ANY SYSTEM

Let us take a moment to summarize the ground we have covered so far. We began with the idea that language was a system for information exchange. Then we considered some reasons for restricting our attention to systems that involve arbitrariness. Following Lewis, we took up a particular proposal about how those systems might look – specifically, the proposal that language is a mapping from sentences into truth conditions, which themselves can be thought of either as sets of possible worlds (propositions) or functions from worlds to truth values.

Importantly, Lewis' definition did not specify precisely what kinds of things should count as *sentences*. The first passage of his that we quoted above mentioned 'certain finite sequences of types of vocal sounds, or of types of inscribable marks'. From this characterization, it seems clear that Lewis is thinking about spoken and written human languages. To deal with the full range of human linguistic forms, the characterization would clearly have to be expanded to cover sign language. But in principle, we can imagine other sorts of arbitrary symbols that could be mapped to truth conditions in ways that would otherwise meet his characterization of language, too.

Consider, for example, the case of the American revolutionary Paul Revere, which Lewis himself describes in his book *Convention*. According to legend, which appears to have a reasonably strong claim to historical accuracy, Revere agreed with Robert Newman and John Pulling that if the British military were to approach by land, the two of them would hang one lantern in a church tower in Boston, and if the approach were to be made by sea, they would hang two lanterns. The British approached by sea, Newman and Pulling lit and hung two lanterns, and Revere was able to warn the militia at Concord in time.

Here it seems like we have an arbitrary symbol – two lit lanterns – being mapped to truth conditions by a system Revere, Newman, and Pulling agreed on. Although we wouldn't ordinarily speak of a lantern's being true or false, in this case it seems appropriate to think in those terms. After all, if a British spy had discovered the system and been able to intervene, they might have thrown off Revere's plans by extinguishing one of the lanterns and thus sending a false message to the effect that the British army would approach by land.

Should we count this lantern system as a language, then? What about flag systems as they are used by sailors to send messages to nearby ships, or the symbols credulous people on the internet sometimes claim thieves use make on peoples' front doors to encode information about which houses it would be good to rob, which are not worth the trouble, and which are too dangerous?

Most philosophers will probably see little harm in using the word 'language' in a loose sense to include systems like these. After all, they involve arbitrary symbols and a mapping that takes those symbols and results in truth conditions (e.g., the set of worlds in which a certain ship is moving to port, or a certain house is not worth robbing). As it turns out, however, there is fairly broad agreement among philosophers (and linguists, for that matter) about a number of other properties that characterize human languages. For the purposes of the philosophy of language, then, and thus of this book, we will take language to involve several further key features.

First, we will look at a property philosophers call **productivity**, and then we will see how it has led people to think that human languages involve a **recursive syntax** and a **compositional semantics**.

1.2.1 PRODUCTIVITY

When introducing the productivity of natural languages – English, Tagalog, Kichwa, and so on – linguists and philosophers often present whacky sentences that they imagine readers will not have encountered ever before. Here is one I came across recently, which I hope you will not already have seen: 'a Queens man was indicted Thursday for allegedly making hush money payments to a porn star shortly before he was elected president of the United States in 2016'.

Before reporter Ryan Schwach generated this sentence in his article for the *Queens Daily Eagle* 'Queens man indicted' on March 30, 2023, I imagine that no one had ever encountered it before. Even if you happen to have already seen this sentence, though, the point it's supposed to make is not ruined. Think about ways you might expand upon it to make new versions. You might say 'A Queens man famous for his love of Kentucky Fried Chicken was indicted…' or 'A Queens man with a distinctive haircut famous for…', and so on.

The 'Queens man' sentence and permutations on it reveal some remarkable things about human languages and about our knowledge of them. First, anyone who knows English will, upon seeing these sentences, immediately recognize that they are sentences of English. In some sense, although no one had ever uttered or written them, they either were already parts of English, or became such immediately upon being produced.

Second, anyone who knows English will, upon seeing one of these sentences, immediately know *what* they mean. As we said above, listeners cannot simply in virtue of knowing English know whether or not a sentence is true, but linguistic knowledge does guarantee they will know *how the world would have to be* in order for the sentence to be true. In possible worlds terms, any English speaker will be able, given any intelligible description of a possible world, to say whether it's a world that makes a certain sentence true or a world that makes the sentence false. And, as we just saw when we expanded on the 'Queens man sentence', these remarkable capacities we have for recognizing and understanding sentences are themselves mirrored by our capacity to generate sentences in our language that others will recognize and understand.

We might call these the two faces of productivity – on the one hand, natural languages appear to be unboundedly large in terms of the sentences that they involve, and on the other, unboundedly large in terms of the meanings they comprise. If a language like English can be thought of as a function, then, as Lewis surmised, it is a function that is defined over unboundedly many inputs and outputs.

1.2.2 RECURSIVE SYNTAX

The fact that human language users are able to grasp such functions tells us some important things. First, think about the input side – the sentences of the language. We are finite creatures. Our brains are capable of storing a large amount of information, at least compared to some of the other kinds of information storage systems we frequently encounter in the world. But that amount is not infinite. This means that our ability to recognize and understand sentences cannot be the result, for example, of our having stored somewhere inside us an infinitely long list of all the sentences of English, which we consult whenever we encounter a candidate sentence in the wild. In addition to the fact that we wouldn't have space inside, this procedure would take too long; our recognition that a certain sequence of sounds is a sentence of a language we know, and our understanding of those sentences, happens very fast.

If we don't have an infinitely long look-up table with all the sentences, though, how are we able to produce and identify so many of them? The best answer that anyone has come up with is that our capacity for recognizing and producing the sentences of the languages we know must be a capacity that is the result of a process that can be described in a compact way finite terms. In the terms linguists and philosophers employ, sentences of natural languages are said to be generated by a finite set of rules that are **recursive**.

A recursive rule is a rule that can take its own outputs as inputs. Consider, for example, the following rule for constructing sentences of English: the result of applying the words 'It is not the case that' to any sentence of English is itself a sentence of English. Now suppose we accept that the sentence 'It is raining' is a sentence of English. On that assumption, our rule will allow us to generate infinitely many new sentences. We start with 'It is raining', and then we apply the rule to get: 'it is not the case that it is raining'. The rule tells us that this, too, is a sentence of English, which means that we can apply it again to get: 'it is not the case that it is not the case that it is raining'.

Although our 'It is not the case' rule will obviously not produce the interestingly infinite variety of sentences we see in natural language, it illustrates the point that it is possible to provide a finite specification of a procedure that will generate infinitely many outputs. One of the major branches of linguistics, syntax, consists in the attempt to specify the rules that in fact are used to generate the grammatical sentences of English (and other languages). Although there isn't time or space here to survey their work, the basic idea is that part of what we know when we know a language is a list of words. It's a long list, but hardly infinite – maybe somewhere in the 10,000–30,000 range. The list is divided into grammatical categories, specifying whether a certain word is a noun, a transitive verb, an intransitive verb, an adjective, and so on.

In addition to this list, which linguists would call the **lexicon**, we know a set of rules for forming sentences, which are defined over grammatical categories. This rulebook for sentence formation is called the grammar or the **syntax** of the language. Consider the following toy syntax:

Rule 1: A noun on its own is a noun phrase (NP)
Rule 2: Adding an adjective to the left of an NP results in a NP
Rule 3: Adding an NP to the left of a verb results in a sentence

Together with our previous rule about 'It is not the case that', this little set of rules will already give us much more interesting complexity than our previous attempt did. Suppose that it's written into the lexicon that 'Ann' is a noun and that 'sleeps' is a verb. So by rule 1, and rule 3, we know that 'Ann sleeps' is a sentence. If we wanted to get infinitely many variations on this sentence, we could of course add our old rule about 'It is not the case that' to the rulebook to get: 'It is not the case that Ann sleeps' and all of the possible expansions thereof. But the grammar specified above would also allow us to do more interesting things. Suppose the lexicon for our language is just the English lexicon, so that we know, for example, that 'clever' is an adjective, 'tall' is an adjective, and so on. By rule 2 from our grammar, we know that 'clever Ann' is an NP. Thus, by rules 1 and 3 again, we can derive the result that 'Clever Ann sleeps' is a sentence. The same procedure will generate 'Tall, clever Ann sleeps', 'Tall, confident, clever Ann sleeps', and so on.

Of course, actually describing the rules that govern a natural language is not going to be easy, and several generations of linguists following the original attempts along these lines that were made by

Noam Chomsky in the late 1950s have spent their careers trying. But in principle, the idea of recursion makes it possible to see how the story might go.

1.2.3 COMPOSITIONAL SEMANTICS

So much for the input side of the language function – the specification of the sentences. Now let's look at the output side – the specification of meanings. Very similar considerations to those we have just looked at for sentences apply in the case of meanings.

In addition to our almost miraculous ability to immediately recognize an unbounded variety of sentences of our language, we have the further ability to immediately see what they mean. As before, this ability seems to impose a clear constraint on the way it must be realized in us. Either we have an unboundedly long list of meanings stored somewhere (to go with the unboundedly large number of sentences whose meanings we know), or we have a procedure defined that allows us to build arbitrarily many meanings out of some finitely specifiable description of their components. Since our minds our finite, the latter explanation seems like it must be the right one.

There is an area at the intersection of linguistics and philosophy called **semantics** (sometimes 'truth-conditional semantics', 'formal semantics', 'linguistic semantics', and similar.) that aims at describing such a procedure. If we accept, as we have for the purposes of this book, that sentence meanings are truth conditions – sets of possible worlds, or functions from possible worlds to truth values – then the semanticist's job is to show how we build truth conditions out of some more fundamental kinds of meaningful elements.

The basic approach semanticists take is very similar to the approach we sketched above in the case of syntax. There, we made use of a large, but nevertheless finite lexicon in which information about a word's grammatical category is stored, together with a rulebook that explains how to put words from different grammatical categories together to make sentences. Here, we see the same distinction – giving a semantics for a natural language involves giving a specification of the meanings of individual words, together with a specification of the rules that allow us to put the words together in a way that will result in truth conditions for sentences. The key idea is that when two words are joined into a larger complex by a syntactic rule, their meanings also form a complex – this process is called **semantic composition**, and the property of languages whose meanings are built this way **compositionality**.

An analogy with chemistry might help to bring this out. Think of what happens when we want to synthesize a complex molecule. In the ideal case for our analogy, we'd start with two elements, which we bond into a compound. Then we combine that compound with another, which itself was formed from two (or more) elements, and so on until we have the sophisticated molecule we want. The staggering diversity of molecules that can be formed on the basis of the elements listed on the periodic table illustrates the productivity made possible by recombining a finite set of elements according to a finite set of rules.

Like the chemist who can synthesize a huge variety of very complicated molecules using a very small number of elements and laws that govern how those elements combine, speakers of a language can produce and interpret a huge variety of sentences simply by knowing the meanings of the words of their language – there are a lot of words, but not nearly as many as there are sentences – and a fairly small number of rules that explain how word meanings can be combined to build larger meaningful elements. We won't look in detail here at what how semantic composition works, but as you may have guessed, it's all about functions and arguments!

1.3 SUMMING UP AND LOOKING FORWARD

Let's take stock of what we have done so far. We began with the idea that language is a system for communication. After considering some communication systems that didn't seem properly linguistic – involving severed heads and open office blinds – we refined our definition to include the property of arbitrariness. We looked in detail at a proposal from David Lewis that aimed to capture arbitrariness by saying that a language is a mapping from symbols to truth conditions, and we looked at some intuitive reasons for thinking that Lewis' characterization made sense (since it seems like when we know a language, we know what would make various sentences true).

Now we have added some further constraints to Lewis' definition by specifying that the kind of languages we care about – the ones people know – are productive; the function they involve maps unboundedly many sentences into unboundedly many truth conditions. And we saw reasons for thinking that productivity is best explained by a language's having a recursive syntax and a compositional semantics.

This is the basic picture against which everything else that we look at in this book will be set. But before we move on to look at the kinds of debates philosophers have had about language in this context, we should go back to the beginning and ask: what happened to communication? We started with the idea that language is a system for communication. We walked through all of these different refinements of the idea that language is a system, looked at what kind of system it is, how it is structured, etc. But none of those refinements obviously have to do with communication – that is, what we actually use language to *do*.

Let us now return to that question and ask: how does knowing a procedure for putting word meanings together in a way that will make truth conditions for sentences allow us to exchange information with each other?

Our old friend David Lewis, again, has an answer that is widely accepted in different forms among philosophers:

> What is language? A social phenomenon which is part of the natural history of human beings; a sphere of human action, wherein people utter strings of vocal sounds, or inscribe strings of marks, and wherein people respond by thought or action to the sounds or marks which they observe to have been so produced.

> This verbal activity is, for the most part, rational. He who produces certain sounds or marks does so for a reason. He knows that someone else, upon hearing his sounds or seeing his marks, is apt to form a certain belief or act in a certain way. He wants, for some reason, to bring about that belief or action. Thus his beliefs and desires give him a reason to produce the sounds or marks, and he does. He who responds to the sounds or marks in a certain way also does so for a reason. He knows how the production of sounds or marks depends upon the producer's state of mind. When he observes the sounds or marks, he is therefore in a position to infer something about the producer's state of mind. He can probably also infer something about the

conditions which caused that state of mind. He may merely come to believe these conclusions, or he may act upon them in accordance with his other beliefs and his desires.

(Lewis 1975, 3-4)

Earlier, Lewis said that a language is an abstract object, a way of mapping arbitrary symbols into truth conditions. Here, Lewis says that a language is a social practice, whereby speakers produce certain sounds and listeners respond by thinking or acting in a certain way. Importantly, the production of sounds on the part of speakers and the thoughts or actions that result on the part of listeners are regular, Lewis thinks, in important ways. Specifically, he thinks that when we share a language with someone, we share a certain kind of **convention**: the convention of only saying things we think are true, and of trusting that other people will do the same.

Of course, this doesn't mean that everyone always speaks the truth or always assumes that others are speaking the truth. But our ability to use a language – in the sense of a mapping from arbitrary symbols into truth conditions – to exchange information depends on our assuming that we are generally aiming to say true things. Suppose we shared a mapping, but not a convention of truthfulness or trust. Without a convention of truth-telling, there would be no reason for anyone to take my producing a sound that's true just in case P to be a reason for believing P. The same is true if we only have trust – what would be trusting one another to do? By combining truthfulness and trust, however, we end up with something really useful – we end up making it the case that by producing a sound that's true just only when P, you give me a reason to believe that P.

For the rest of Part One, we will look at three areas in which debates have cropped up concerning some of the details that this picture leaves open. In Chapter Two, we will look at questions about semantics – questions about what the fundamental meanings of certain kinds of expressions are. In Chapter Three, we will look at metasemantic questions – questions about why a certain thing is the meaning of a certain word, instead of some other thing, or nothing at all (questions about how a word gets its meaning, if you like). In Chapter Four, we will look at questions about pragmatics or conversational dynamics – questions about what exactly we are up to when we utter a sentence with certain truth conditions, and how we are able to move from knowledge of truth conditions to knowledge of a broader sort of meaning – that is, to see what people are 'really driving at' when they produce sentences with certain truth conditions.

NOTES

1. Actually, even this much may not be as clear as it seems at first. Most people will say that British and American English are the same language. If someone raised a doubt about this, a standard response would be to point out that for as much comedic mileage as can be gotten out of the differences, most of what most people who identify themselves as British or American English speakers say will be understood by most of the others. But what about Swedish and Norwegian? Most speakers of either of these will say that they are different languages, but much of what most speakers of either say will be understood without great difficulty by most speakers of the other. Some report that things go the other way around with spoken Arabic.

2. As we will see later on, there might be more to knowing a language than knowing what the truth conditions associated with sentences of it are, but. However at the very least, this seems to be both a minimal requirement, and to capture quite a bit of our ordinary notion.

3. However, it is important to emphasize that it is not quite the case that anything goes where worlds are concerned. Things that involve logical contradictions are ruled out – so there are no worlds with round squares, or where 2 and 2 make 5. That said, there may be worlds in which we use the shape '5' to represent the number 4, so that when kids write '2+2=5' on their answer papers, the teacher gives them credit. If it seems like you can imagine a world in which 2 and 2 make 5, most philosophers think what you are really imagining is a case like the one I just described.

4. You may wonder: 'what about worlds in which there are no cities in Madagascar? Or worlds in which there is no Madagascar?' These are questions we will set aside here.

FURTHER READING

The discussion in this chapter draws less directly on a specific philosophical literature than the discussion in the remaining chapters will. The central sources I've used from philosophy are:

- David Lewis. "Languages and language". In: *Minnesota Studies in the Philosophy of Science*. Ed. by Keith Gunderson. University of Minnesota Press, 1975, pp. 3–35.
- David Lewis. *Convention: A Philosophical Study*. Cambridge, MA: Harvard University Press, 1969.

For a sense of how the topics presented here are approached in linguistics, I can recommend:

- Maggie Tallerman. *Understanding Syntax*. Routledge, 2020.
- Irene Heim and Angelika Kratzer. *Semantics in Generative Grammar*. Oxford, UK: Blackwell, 1998.

For more detail on some of the philosophical themes touched upon here, I recommend also:

- Menzel, Christopher, "Possible Worlds", The Stanford Encyclopedia of Philosophy (Fall 2023 Edition), Edward N. Zalta & Uri Nodelman (eds.)
- Speaks, Jeff, "Theories of Meaning", The Stanford Encyclopedia of Philosophy (Spring 2021 Edition), Edward N. Zalta (ed.)

SEMANTICS

In Chapter One, we developed the idea that natural languages, like Pashto, Walpiri, and so on, are abstract objects: functions from sentences to truth conditions. That idea allowed us to get a grip on how people can use language to exchange information – if you and I both know the same mapping from sentences to truth conditions, and I take you to produce sentences only when you think they're true, then if you say 'it's raining', I can come to know that it is raining (or at least, that you think it is).

With those two key pieces of the philosophical background on the table, we are now in a position to start to look at some of the detailed questions that have been the focus of disputes in the philosophy of language. If you found Chapter One difficult, don't despair – although the philosophy of language does involve some notoriously abstract topics, from here on out things will be a bit more concrete than they were at the beginning, and we'll have more specific examples to sink our teeth into than we did while setting things up.

The group of questions that will be the focus of this chapter are questions about **semantics** – questions, that is, about what different expressions mean. Sometimes people say 'Ah, that's just semantics!' when they want to dismiss a dispute as merely verbal; here we'll see that questions about semantics can actually run quite deep!

DOI: 10.4324/9781003250753-2

At the end of Chapter One, we looked at reasons for thinking that natural languages have the property of compositionality. We said, that is, that the meanings of natural language sentences are constructed by taking the meanings of their basic parts (words, or maybe even pieces of words like suffixes and prefixes) and combining them according to a relatively small number of rules (small, at least, compared to the number of sentences we can understand). We know from the work we did in that chapter that the meanings of sentences are supposed to be truth conditions. But that leaves us with quite a bit of lee-way with regard to how we think about the meanings of the parts that make sentences up (and with regard to how we think about the rules of composition, for that matter, although we will focus our dis-cussion here on debates about the meanings of particular classes of expressions).

Our aim in this chapter will not be to defend a particular view about what the meaning of any particular sort of expression is. Instead, we aim to introduce some of the major positions that have been developed in the philosophical literature and to give you a sense of the ways in which philosophers have argued for those positions, that is, of the *kinds* of considerations philosophers think support one view or another. We'll consider the chapter a success if after reading it, you're in a position to give a philosophical argument in support of a semantic position of your own.

2.1 PROPER NAMES

For historical, pedagogical, and philosophical reasons, a good place to start on this task is a long-standing debate about proper names; if you were to take a course in the philosophy of language at a research university in the US or UK, this is almost certainly the material you'd cover in the first few lectures. We won't spend a lot of time trying to give a criterion for picking proper names out from among other words in a language – it'll be enough for us to rely on the kind of definition you might have heard in grade school, along the lines of 'a proper name refers to a specific person or place, and in English, is written with a capital letter'. Of course, there are examples of things that seem like proper names that don't meet this definition, like 'e.e. cumming' and 'bell hooks'. But this description will get you on to the basic phenomenon well enough – think of 'Aristotle', 'Barack Obama', 'Antananarivo', and so on. Proper names are sometimes contrasted with ordinary nouns, which do not pick out a specific individual, like 'cat', 'capital city', or 'lettuce'. And sometimes they are contrasted with a class of expressions philosophers call 'definite descriptions', which might pick out a single individual, but seem to do so by different means from a name; for example, 'the President of the United States', 'the tallest mountain in South America', 'the first dog born at sea in the 20th century', and so on. (We'll talk more about descriptions later on, and even see that some philosophers think names and descriptions are not really as different as they might appear.)

2.1.1   A SIMPLE SEMANTICS FOR NAMES

Have you thought before about what the meaning of a name is? If you take a particular name and search for it on the internet, you might see things like "'Bertha' is an Old German name that means 'bright'". The relationship between the property of brightness, however, and people named 'Bertha' is not very clear. Usually, parents pick a name before they've had a chance to learn what their child is like, so it doesn't seem plausible to think the choice reflects the child's nature (maybe the opposite sounds more plausible – that parents pick a name in the vague hope that the choice will confer some properties on the child). It seems instructive, moreover, that for most names, you only learn their 'meaning', in this sense, when you look them up. (Maybe you know the 'meaning' of your own name – but how many others would you know without looking?) While there are certain names that have equivalents in other languages – Biblical names, for example – we don't normally, when learning a language, learn how to translate names. So, while you might wonder how you should pronounce 'Ciaran' when speaking Korean or Ukrainian, it seems like it would be a strange question to ask what the Korean name for 'Ciaran' is. Similarly, when you learn a foreign language, you might learn what kinds of names are typical – in some languages, there are quite specific rules about name formation, and in some, a finite list – but you don't, in addition to having to learn how to say 'water' and 'airplane' and so on, have to learn the names.

One way of explaining this would be to say that names don't really *have* meanings in the same way that common nouns, verbs, adjectives, and so on have meanings. In fact, many philosophers have endorsed a view like that. On what is often called a 'Millian' semantics for names, after an early proponent, John Stuart Mill, the meaning of a name is said to be just the object it picks out. On this view, the meaning of the name 'Barack Obama' is the person, Barack Obama. The meaning of the name 'Antananarivo' is the city, Antananarivo. The meaning of the name 'the San José Sharks' is just the hockey team.

This last example shows that some things that look like descriptions – expressions that begin with the word 'the' – might really be names. How do we know when we're looking at a name and when we are looking at a description? Again, we won't really worry too much about this distinction for now, but a quick rule of thumb would be that a description picks out whatever it does *in virtue of describing it*. Names, however, don't seem, at least on the face of things, to work like this – as is held by an old joke mentioned by the philosopher Saul Kripke in work we will look at soon, the Holy Roman empire was neither holy, nor Roman, nor an empire.

One argument in favor of Millianism about names is its simplicity. Other things being equal, philosophers tend to prefer simpler theories over more complex ones. So, if there isn't obvious explanatory work to be done by whatever sense of meaning the association between brightness and the name 'Bertha' is supposed to do, there isn't anything to be gained by saying 'Bertha' means brightness. And there may be something lost – you certainly can't walk into a well-lit room and say 'Wow, it's really Bertha in here, can someone turn the lights down a bit?', as we might expect you to be able to do if 'Bertha' really meant the same thing as 'bright'.

Another argument for the simple view is that it seems to make the right predictions about some key data involving names. Recall that we said previously that we will take the meanings of sentences to be their truth conditions. And that we assume that those meanings are derived compositionally from the meanings of the sentences' parts. As philosophers, we don't have any special instruments that detect word meanings in the way a scale detects the mass of objects placed on it or an oscilloscope detects sound waves. People who know a language, however, usually have pretty clear intuitions about the truth conditions of the sentences they encounter. It is standard practice in philosophy to take those intuitions for granted and work our way backwards from them to try and figure out what the meanings of individual words must be.[1]

Suppose, for example, that you want to figure out what proper names in English mean. You could do worse than to start by looking at the intuitions some sentences involving names elicit. Consider, for example:

(1)   Ronald Reagan was once the President of the United States.

(2)   Margaret Thatcher was once the President of the United States.

Here we have two sentences, one true and one false. We can see that the only difference in the sentences is a difference in the name that occupies the subject position – in the first sentence, that name is 'Ronald Reagan' and in the second, 'Margaret Thatcher '. This suggests that any difference in the truth values of the two sentences is caused by a difference in the meanings of the two names.

Think about the truth conditions of the two sentences. Intuitively, the first sentence seems to be true in all the worlds where Reagan was once president, and the second in all the worlds where Thatcher was. So, if we think about worlds in which Reagan is president and has a dog, those seem like sentences in which (1) would be true. The same goes for worlds where Reagan won the election but has no dog, and worlds where he won and has both a dog and a cat, and so on. It does not seem likely to be an accident, then, that the sentence that features the name 'Ronald Reagan' depends for its truth on how things are with a certain person – Reagan – and the sentence that has the name 'Margaret Thatcher' depends for its truth on how things are with a different person – Thatcher. A plausible explanation for these differences is that the meaning of the name 'Ronald Reagan' is the man, Ronald Reagan, while the meaning of the name 'Margaret Thatcher' is the woman, Margaret Thatcher.

Further support for this idea can be had by considering some more sentences:

(3) Joe Biden wears Ray-Ban aviator sunglasses.

(4) Joe Biden likes ice cream.

(5) Joe Biden drives a Corvette.

Think about the truth conditions associated with these sentences. Each involves quite different properties – when we think about the worlds that will verify or falsify the sentences, we have to look at patterns involving sunglasses, ice cream, and Corvettes. But there is also something importantly similar across these possibilities – in each one, it's the question of how things are with a certain guy (Joe Biden), that matters, that is, with Joe Biden. Why is he always the one we have to look at? A natural explanation would be that it's because the name that appears in each of these sentences, 'Joe Biden', has him as its meaning.

2.1.2 FREGE'S PUZZLE

Gottlob Frege, a late 19th and early 20th-century philosopher considered by many to be one of the founders not only of the philosophy of language but also of analytic philosophy itself, thought the simple view of names was wrong.

Frege made his case using a deceptively simple-looking argument. Consider the following pair of sentences:

(6) Hesperus is Hesperus.

(7) Hesperus is Phosphorus.

'Hesperus' and 'Phosphorus' are two names for the same thing, the planet Venus. So, Frege reasoned, if the meaning of a name is just the object named, these sentences should have the same meaning. But do they?

Frege thinks they do not. He says that (6) is an **a priori** or **analytic** truth – anyone can see just from looking at it, that is, that it is true. But (7) certainly does not appear to have this property. In fact, Frege says, it took years of astronomical observations and theory building for people to realize that the object they had been calling

'Phosphorus' (the last star-looking thing that is visible in the morning sky when all the rest have faded) was the very same object as the object they had been calling 'Hesperus' (the first star-looking thing to become visible in the sky as it grows dark in the evening).

Frege took sentences like (6) and (7) – which he called **identity statements** – to show that there must be more to the meaning of a name than the object it names. Before we look at what that something more is, though, it's worth taking a moment to emphasize that Frege does not want to deny that *part* of the meaning of a name is the object named.

On Frege's picture, names involve two levels of meaning, with the object picked out by a name counting as its meaning at one level. Frege calls this the level of **reference** and philosophers nowadays, whether they agree with Frege's two-level theory of meaning or not, often say things like 'the **referent** of the name "Joe Biden" is Joe Biden'. In this terminology, we might say that the simple view of names that we began with is the view that the meaning of a name is exhausted by its reference.

In its English translation, the paper in which Frege develops his famous two-level theory is called 'On sense and reference'. Reference, as we just saw, is the level of meaning involving the object picked out by a name. The other level of meaning, then, is one that Frege calls the level of **sense**. So what is the level of sense about?

Answering this question is not quite as straightforward as we would like. There's no passage in Frege's work where he writes anything like 'the sense of the name "Hesperus" is … ' and then fills in the dots with exactly what he takes the sense of the name 'Hesperus' to be. He does, however, tell us quite a bit about the theoretical roles the notion of sense is supposed to play, which allows us to get a decent handle on the idea. Consider the following passage, for example:

> Let *a, b, c* be the lines connecting the vertices of a triangle with the midpoints of the opposite sides. The point of intersection of *a* and *b* is then the same as the point of intersection of *b* and *c*. So we have different designations for the same point, and these names ('point of intersection of *a* and *b*', 'point of intersection of *b* and *c*') likewise indicate the mode of presentation.
> (Frege 1892/1948, 210)

Two interrelated ways of thinking about sense come out in this passage. One is that the sense of an expression **determines its referent**. Another is that the sense of an expression is a **mode of presentation** of an object.

An analogy with travel directions can help to bring out what the reference-determining role comes to. Directions tell us how to get to a certain destination; if you have good directions that start at the place you are, and you follow them correctly, you'll end up at the place they specify. Of course, it's only rarely the case that there would be a single set of directions for reaching a certain destination. If you walk, you might follow one path, and another if you cycle. You might choose to take the quickest path, or the path that is least steep, or the path that is most scenic.

As in the case of directions, the sense associated with an expression tells us how to find a certain object in the world. And as in the case of directions, there may be multiple routes that lead to the same place. We can find our way to the same point in Frege's triangle either by drawing line *a* and then line *b* and seeing where they intersect or by drawing line *b* and then line *c* and seeing where they intersect. We can imagine many other routes that would lead us to that point instead of any of the other points contained within the boundaries of the triangle; if we had a very precise ruler, we might specify the point's distance along one of the lines *a, b, or c*, or we could invoke its distance from some other point, itself picked out in any number of ways, or we could specify other lines through the triangle in terms of their relation to its vertices, or whatever.

To put this thought in classically Fregean terms, philosophers often say that expressions that have different senses can nevertheless share a referent. So, the descriptions 'the intersection of *a* and *b*' and 'the intersection of *b* and *c*' have different senses, but the same referent. The converse, however, is not true – as you may have guessed, any two expressions that share a sense will inevitably also share a referent – to invoke our analogy once more, if you follow instructions that say to get on the 59 bus at London's Euston Station and you get off at the seventh stop, you'll be at Aldwych, no matter whether those instructions are written on a piece of paper, or your phone, or if they were revealed to you in a dream.

In addition to reference-fixing, the triangle example brings out another role Fregean senses play. Frege and his commentators often talk about how different senses involve different modes of presentation, or ways of thinking of an object. Even if the point that is picked out by intersecting lines *a* and *b* is the same point as the point picked out by intersecting lines *b* and *c*, that is, intuitively it seems like those two descriptions present that point in a different light, or under different 'guises', as you will sometimes hear philosophers saying.

To take a less abstract example, think of the particular way in which someone might be presented to you the first time you meet – if your first encounter takes place at a work event, you might be introduced to them in terms of their professional role, like 'head of marketing' or 'internal affairs lead'. If you meet the same person for the first time in a social context, you might be introduced to them as 'Amin's partner' or 'Ari's cousin'. While these might be ways of thinking of the same person, they are different in terms of which features they make salient. A friend who worked as a substitute teacher at an elementary school once told me a story about running into one of her students' families in the grocery store after dinner. Visibly disoriented, the student asked 'But shouldn't you be at school?' One way to understand the student's confusion might be to say that while they recognized my friend, they were used to thinking of her under a certain guise – as someone who does certain things in the classroom – and weren't expecting to be confronted with the same person presented differently.

The idea that we can think of the same object in different ways is a key piece of Frege's theory, and in a moment we'll look at how it helps him address the puzzle involving Hesperus and Phosphorus. But first it's worth taking a moment to make sure we don't get carried away in over-individualizing senses. Suppose I tell you to think of Barack Obama. You may think of a particular occasion on which you saw him on TV, or think of him as the person whose face is on Shepard Fairy's famous poster, or in any number of other ways. Each of those ways will elicit different sets of associations, emotions, memories, and so on for you than it does for me or for anyone else. Frege calls differences like these differences in the **ideas** associated with an expression, and he takes care to distinguish them from senses, which are supposed to be shared by everyone who grasps an expression. So while the description 'the intersection of lines *a* and *b*' may feel different to someone who likes geometry and someone who doesn't, and while it reminds me of the whirl of the fan of an overhead projector in a darkened classroom in the early summer, but may not do that for you, there is something that all of us who speak English have in common when we think about an object *as* the object that lies at that intersection.

Frege provides an example to illustrate this point:

> The following analogy will perhaps clarify these relationships. Somebody observes the Moon through a telescope. I compare the Moon itself to the referent; it is the object of the observation, mediated by the real image projected by the object glass in the interior of the telescope, and by the retinal image of the observer. The former I compare to the sense, the latter is like the idea.
>
> (Frege 1892/1948, 213)

Senses, then, are ways of thinking, but ways that many people can share, while ideas are the subjective reactions or specific thoughts that a certain individual has when thinking about something or someone. While we might all be struck differently by the Shepard Fairey poster, remember seeing it in the different places we did, etc., anytime any of us think of Obama *as* the guy from the poster, there is (arguably) something in common our thoughts have.

To invoke one final analogy that might help bring this kind of commonality out, consider the perspective one gains on a landscape when it is seen from a certain point of view. Take, for example, the view of the Kowloon peninsula from Lion Peak in Hong Kong, or Independence Square from the Hotel Ukraine in Kyiv. The view will be different on different days, as the weather varies, the season, the time of day, and so on. And of course, it may be that different people have different experiences while taking it in; what might look to a tourist to be an undifferentiated mass of buildings might look different to a local who knows the different areas, has different memories of each, with associated emotional resonances and so on. If some of the stranger possibilities countenanced in the philosophy of mind obtain, it might even be that your qualitative experience of seeing the sky and the water is somehow intrinsically different from the qualitative experience I have when viewing them in the same conditions. Still, there seems to be a minimal sense in which two people who stand at that place and look in that direction share something – a perspective, determined by physics, geometry, geography, and so on.

With this characterization of sense on the table, let's go back and see how Frege approaches the puzzle we began with, that is, the puzzle of explaining the difference in the intuitions our Hesperus and Phosphorus sentences (repeated here) generate:

(6)   Hesperus is Hesperus.

(7)   Hesperus is Phosphorus.

The first step in giving a Fregean analysis of the difference in our reactions to these sentences is to note that Frege thinks names, like the descriptions we used in the triangle examples, have both a sense and a reference. As we saw when introducing sentences (6) and (7) , the two names involved have the same referent – both pick out the planet Venus. But as our discussion of the triangle makes clear, having the same referent doesn't necessarily mean that two expressions have the same sense.

This makes it possible for Frege to explain the difference in our reactions to (6) and (7) by saying that 'Hesperus' presents Venus in one way, and 'Phosphorus' in another. Roughly, we might try to capture the sense of 'Hesperus' by comparing it to the sense of the description 'the brightest visible body in the sky in the early evening'. On the other hand, the sense of 'Phosphorus' is something like the sense of the description 'the brightest visible body in the sky in the late morning'.

The fact that the same object, Venus, can be presented in these two different ways – as the object that's so bright in the evening sky that it's visible before any other, and as the object that's so bright in the morning sky that it remains visible after the others have all faded – explains why (6) is obvious and (7) is not. It's a bit like if our uttering (6) and (7) was really equivalent to:

(8)   The brightest object in the early evening sky is the brightest object in the early evening sky.

(9)   The brightest object in the early evening sky is the brightest object in the late morning sky.

I say 'a bit like' because Frege never actually says that the sense of a name is equivalent to a description, or even that it is equivalent to the sense of a description. Getting more precise about this would require really getting into gritty details of Frege interpretation that go beyond the scope of our presentation here; for our purposes, the comparison to descriptions is safe as long as we remember that it isn't quite Frege's final answer.

In summary, then, Frege offers an argument against the simple view of names, together with a positive view of his own. To the level of reference that the simple view took to exhaust the meaning of a name, Frege added another layer of meaning, which he says both determines the referent and explains the cognitive significance of a name.

2.1.3 KRIPKE'S CRITIQUE OF DESCRIPTIVISM

Views about the semantics of names that have a broadly Fregean structure — views that hold that part of the meaning of a name is something like a description that the name's referent satisfies — are sometimes called **descriptivist** views. Although there are still philosophers who endorse versions of descriptivism, many take Saul Kripke, another prominent figure in analytic philosophy, to have provided compelling arguments against them. In a series of lectures at Princeton University in 1970 that were later published in the form of a book called *Naming and Necessity*, Kripke offered several arguments designed to show that a version of the Millian view of names that we began this section with must be right after all. We will consider three of those arguments here.

Kripke's first argument challenges the idea that our ability to refer to an object using a name is an ability we have in virtue of our associating anything like a Fregean sense with the name. If we say, with Frege, that the sense of a name fixes its referent, it might seem like we'd have to say that in order for a person to be able to use a certain name to pick out a certain object, they would have to know what the name's sense is. But if sense is something like a recipe for finding an object in the world, how many of us would be able to provide such a recipe?

In a presentation that demonstrates quite a clever sense of humor, Kripke asks us to think about who we take ourselves to be talking about when we talk about Einstein, Gödel, and other famous people we have never met. Most of us, he presumes, have the intuition that when we use the name 'Einstein' we are talking about Einstein, that when we use the name 'Gödel', we are talking about Gödel, and so on. But, Kripke argues, very few of us would be in a position to provide anything like a description that would uniquely pick out Einstein.

Think of the kinds of attempts people might make to analyze 'Einstein' in terms of a description if they had to. Someone might say: 'Einstein is the person who proposed the theory of relativity'. That would be right, although probably not very many users of the term 'Einstein' would be able to say much about the theory of relativity in any detail. I myself would probably mumble something about $E = mc^2$ and maybe give some kind of vague analogy involving passengers on a train tossing balls in the air, but beyond that, I suspect like many others I would fall back on something like 'well, it's the theory Einstein came up with'. This makes it seem implausible to think that my ability to refer to Einstein – an ability few people would doubt I have – is an ability I have in virtue of my being in possession of some uniquely identifying description of the man.

The point can be sharpened if we consider Kripke's allegation that many people would in fact say something like 'Einstein is the person who invented the atomic bomb'. This is a description that doesn't plausibly point in the direction of Einstein at all – if the description picks out anyone uniquely, it presumably picks out Oppenheimer, or someone who worked under him. Still, Kripke says, people who think it was Einstein that invented the bomb and say things like 'It would have been better if Einstein hadn't invented the bomb at all' are plausibly nevertheless saying things about Einstein. If we hear someone say 'Einstein invented the bomb', we might reply 'That's false, it was Oppenheimer', which suggests we take them to be saying something false about Einstein.

Some philosophers have offered theories that are Fregean in spirit, but which attempt to dodge the problem of no one's being able to give a good individuating description of Einstein by loosening Frege's ideal that there should be a single sense associated with a single name. Kripke points to John Searle, for example, as someone who thought that while ordinary speakers may not be able to come up with any single description that would pick out the person we intuitively think should be picked out by means of a certain name, they would be generally able to come up with a *cluster* of descriptions that together would do the job. We can imagine a version of Frege's view being constructed like this – instead of saying that names have a single sense, we could say that they're associated with a cluster or cloud of senses and that the referent of a name is the object that satisfies most or some appropriately weighted subset of them. For Einstein, maybe the cluster might include properties like the property of being famous, of being a physicist, of having unkempt white hair, of having been born in Germany, and so on.

> What do you think? Could the cluster theory defeat Kripke's first objection?

Kripke's second argument against descriptivism concerns questions about possibility and necessity. Philosophers call these **modal** questions, and this argument is often called Kripke's **modal argument**. To see how the modal argument works, recall the notion of possible worlds that we introduced in Chapter One. There we said that a possible world is a way things might be and that there are as many of them as there are ways we can imagine things being. We can imagine, for example, a world basically just like ours but in which during the 1968 election for US president, Nixon lost and Humphrey won. We can imagine worlds in which Nixon won and then decided to adopt a dog, worlds in which Nixon won and then decided to adopt a cat, worlds in which Humphrey won and decided to adopt a dog, worlds in which Humphrey won and decided to adopt a cat, and so on.

Now think about the description 'president of the US in 1970'. Just as we can imagine all sorts of different ways a world might be, we can ask which person that description would pick out in each of those worlds. In all the worlds where Humphrey wins, it seems like the description would pick out Humphrey, and in all the worlds where Nixon wins, it would pick out Nixon. Think again about the way we characterized Fregean senses – we said they're like instructions for finding an object. But following the same instructions for finding an object, in worlds where the way things go is different from the way they go here, may very well turn up different things – if you go looking for the person who won the 1968 election in a world where Humphrey won, you'll find Humphrey, and applying that same criterion in a world where Nixon won will give you Nixon.

Although the modal argument involves reasoning about what an expression would pick out in metaphysically possible scenarios, the basic idea that an expression can pick out different things when evaluated with regard to different circumstances does not itself involve any sophisticated philosophical machinery. Think about descriptions like 'the tallest person in the room' or 'the oldest house on the block'. In different rooms or on different blocks, these descriptions will pick out different things.

Kripke thinks the flexibility that descriptions involve – their picking out different things in different worlds – makes them different from names, which always pick out the same thing if they pick out anything at all. Consider again the way we described our worlds a minute ago. We said, when describing our first non-actual possibility, that it was a world where Nixon might have lost. As Kripke puts things, this way of speaking suggests that when we use names to talk about the different ways in which things might have gone, we have some kind of direct grasp on the person named, around whom we go on to build out the various scenarios.

This intuition can be brought out more by considering some example sentences:

(10) Nixon might not have been the president in 1970.

(11) Nixon might not have been Nixon.

It seems totally uncontroversial that the sentence 'Nixon might not have been president in 1970' is true. He might have lost! In fact, he only barely carried the popular vote (although he won handily in the electoral college). But the sentence 'Nixon might not have been Nixon' seems like nonsense. What would it even mean to say that he might not have been himself? If we discount metaphorical senses in which 'you're not acting like yourself today' means something like 'you're not acting the way you normally do', then this seems like an obvious contradiction.

Kripke takes this to show that names are not equivalent to descriptions. Descriptions pick out different things in different worlds, and the existence of these worlds makes modal sentences like (10) true – for any property you can think of! But names pick out the same thing in all worlds in which they pick out anything, and this makes sentences like (11) seem necessarily false.

There's one more way of spinning this basic thought that is worth unpacking. Suppose some version of Frege's view of names is true, and part of the meaning of 'Aristotle' is a sense, something we might try to capture with the description 'the teacher of Alexander the Great'. Then it seems like it becomes a necessary truth that Aristotle taught Alexander. In the terms of our possible worlds framework, it'd mean that there is no world, among all the infinite variety of worlds, in which Aristotle failed to teach Alexander. But that seems extremely implausible. Kripke thinks that maybe there is some sense in which you wouldn't have been you if your parents hadn't been born, or if your genes were very different. But intuitively, it seems like for any possible action that you have in fact taken, you could have not taken it, without compromising your identity. I ate cereal this morning, but might not have. I work as a philosophy professor, but might not have. It doesn't seem hard at all to imagine a world in which Aristotle decided not to be a teacher, or in which he died early, or whatever. As Kripke puts things, when we imagine these scenarios, it doesn't seem like we're imagining scenarios in which someone who looks a lot like Aristotle didn't teach. We're imagining scenarios in which the guy – that guy! – didn't teach.

Importantly, Kripke thinks, this line of reasoning will extend to anything you do, or anything anyone does. So, while Searle thinks that the cluster of descriptions associated with your name is such that you could have failed to do all of the things they say you did, he thinks you have to have done at least some of them. But Kripke thinks this is wrong.

Kripke's third argument against descriptivism is an argument about what we can know, and philosophers sometimes call it Kripke's 'epistemic argument'. Kripke asks us to imagine two mathematicians,

Gödel and Schmidt. In actual fact – in our world, that is, the world in which I am writing this book and you are reading it – Gödel proved that arithmetic was incomplete. If there were a Fregean sense associated with the name 'Gödel', it would probably be 'the person who proved that arithmetic was incomplete'. But Kripke invites us to imagine a detective story. Imagine that in the future, historians discover a hidden archive of Gödel's papers, suggesting that all of the work on the proof was actually done by a graduate student, Schmidt. Imagine, furthermore, that Gödel wasn't particularly good at math at all but that he was a very convincing actor and had an incredible memory, so that he could read the manuscripts Schmidt painstakingly prepared and present them as his own work, complete with responses to likely questions, and so on.

Does this seem hard to imagine? Well, on the one hand, everyone will accept that it's an outlandish story; thankfully, things like this don't happen very often. But there don't appear to be any deep conceptual difficulties with the story, right? Anyone who reads it will understand. Kripke takes this to show that Frege's theory is wrong. If Frege's theory were right, the scenario just described should make no sense at all. No one could discover that Gödel actually stole Schmidt's results, because if 'Gödel' has the sense of the description 'the guy who discovered the incompleteness of arithmetic', then we can know, just from looking at the sentence, that Gödel discovered the incompleteness of arithmetic! That sentence should be just as obvious as the sentence 'Hesperus is Hesperus'. Along the same lines we considered in our discussion of the modal problem, it seems clear that we can imagine finding evidence that shows not only that anyone might not have done certain things but that they did not in fact do them. But if this is right, the names we use to talk about the people we talk about aren't names that encode their exploits as part of their meaning or use them to fix their referents.

2.2 DEFINITE DESCRIPTIONS

Historically, much of the philosophy of language descends from discussions about the semantics of two classes of expression – names and definite descriptions. We have had an overview covering some of the major turning points in the literature on names. Now let's turn our attention to definite descriptions.

We can start by taking up the question: what is a definite description? As we did in the case of names, a good first answer involves looking at the phenomenon in rough and ready terms, using a simple grammatical criterion. For our purposes – and for the purposes of quite a bit of work in philosophy, which has tended to focus on English – we'll say that definite descriptions are phrases of the form 'the *F*', where a predicate (a noun, some adjectives together with a noun, etc.) go in the *F*-slot. So, for example, 'the president of the US in 1980', 'the 2023 defensive points leader in the National Hockey League', 'the first dog born at sea in the 20th century', and so on. Note that these are all singular descriptions – while plural definites, like 'the people who had tickets to the free BTS concert in Busan' and 'the authors of *Principia Mathematica*', meet our grammatical criterion, we will set them aside for our purposes here.

What philosophical questions do definite descriptions raise, and what are some of the major philosophical theories of them? As in the case of proper names, most philosophical work on the topic of definite descriptions descends in one way or another from Frege. You may be relieved to hear, in fact, that we have already done nearly all of the work required to put Frege's theory of definite descriptions on the table. That is because, in contrast to the approach we took earlier of using the ordinary schoolroom conception of names to pick out the phenomenon, Frege took a different view. For Frege, the class of expressions that we previously labeled 'proper names' and the class of expressions we've just agreed to call 'definite descriptions' really belonged to one family.

2.2.1 AN EXTENSION OF FREGE'S THEORY

If you remember the basic shape of Frege's analysis of names, you'll be in a good position to appreciate his view of descriptions, too. Frege took both proper names and definite descriptions to work in fundamentally the same way – both have a sense, and both have a reference. Like names, the referent of a definite description is picked out by its sense. Like names, the sense of a definite description provides a mode of presentation of a referent, explains intuitions about what is obvious and what is not, and so on. The major difference is just that unlike 'Bertha', 'Hesperus', and 'Phosphorus', definite descriptions wear their senses on their sleeves, as it were – so the sense of the descriptions 'the brightest object in the evening sky' and 'the brightest object in the morning sky' are obvious in a way the senses of 'Hesperus' and 'Phosphorus' are not.

Among other things, this means that many of the Kripkean objections to Frege's theory of what we called names don't really apply to his theory, understood as a theory of descriptions. For example, while we said there wasn't any obviously publicly available sense for 'Einstein', it seems much more plausible to think that there is such a sense for the description 'the 2023 defensive points leader in the NHL'. That description presents whoever it does as the defensive player who registered the most points in the NHL in 2023. So it doesn't seem unreasonable to think that people who use that expression to talk about a certain person are able to do so in virtue of that person's being the one who satisfies the description, that is, in virtue of their having scored the most points in the NHL among defensemen.

> Frege's view of descriptions manages to avoid Kripke's modal and epistemic arguments against his view of names. Can you see why? How did the modal argument work? Can you reconstruct a version of that argument, but using descriptions instead of names?

2.2.2   RUSSELL'S THEORY OF DESCRIPTIONS

To this day, a version of Frege's treatment of definite descriptions is the standard view among linguists. Philosophers, however, have tended to prefer an alternative that was first proposed in the early 20th century by another person who is widely considered to be another of the founders of analytic philosophy: Bertrand Russell.

Although his work in a wide range of areas of philosophy is pioneering and remains relevant today, one of the innovations Russell is particularly well known for is called the **theory of descriptions**, which turns fundamentally on his analysis of the meaning of the word 'the'. Russell begins the chapter of his *Introduction to Mathematical Philosophy* in which he presents the theory with this amazing passage:

> We dealt in the preceding chapter with the words *all* and *some*; in this chapter we shall consider the word *the* in the singular, and in the next chapter we shall consider the word *the* in the plural. It may be thought excessive to devote two chapters to one word, but to the philosophical mathematician it is a word of very great importance: like Browning's Grammarian with the enclitic δε, I would give the doctrine of this word if I were 'dead from the waist down' and not merely in a prison.
> (Russell 1919, 167)

Russell thought the word 'the' was so important because he thought that by giving a proper analysis of it, an analysis built on powerful logical tools that he and Frege were largely responsible for, we could avoid philosophical traps involving confused thinking that many philosophers have fallen into previously.

To see one of those traps, consider the following famous passage:

> If we say 'the king of England is bald', that ... would seem [to be], not a statement about the complex meaning 'the king of England', but about the actual man denoted by the meaning. But now consider 'the king of France is bald'. By parity of form, this also ought to be about the denotation of the phrase 'the king of France'. But this phrase, though it has a meaning provided 'the king of England' has a meaning, has certainly no denotation, at least in any obvious sense. Hence one would suppose that 'the king of France is bald' ought to be nonsense; but it is not nonsense, since it is plainly false.
> (Russell 1905, 483)

This passage introduces a problem we might call the problem of **empty** or **non-referring descriptions**. The problem is this: it seems obvious that the expression 'the king of England' affects the truth conditions of sentences it occurs in a certain systematic way. Specifically, that expression makes it so that those sentences will be true or false depending on how things are with whoever is king of England at the time of the sentence's being uttered. If someone says 'the king of England is bald', whether they've said something true or false depends on how things are with, at the time of this writing, Charles III.

At the time of this writing, however, and as was true of Russell's time, there is no king of France. So the description 'the king of France' is 'empty' – nothing satisfies it. But, as Russell points out, sentences involving that expression are clearly meaningful – we have no trouble imaging the kinds of scenarios that would make them true, and Russell thinks that the particular sentence he uses in his example is in fact false. If there is no person, however, that is picked out by the description 'the king of France', what could the meaning of the description be? What role could it play in determining the truth conditions of the sentences it occurs in? And how could it play a role in making the sentence 'the king of France is bald' false?

Russell thinks there are two basic strategies one can take in the face of this problem. The first would be to argue that, contrary to appearances, there *is* in fact a referent for the expression 'the king of France', even if it isn't a referent of the same kind as the referent of 'the king of England'. The second is to find a way to say that a description can be meaningful even if it lacks a referent. Russell argues against versions of each strategy before proposing his own version of the second.

The version of the first strategy that Russell considers is one that he attributes to Alexius Meinong. Meinong's view was that there are, in some sense, more objects than the ones that actually exist. So, you and I, and trees and cars, and perhaps numbers and concepts exist. In addition to the objects that exist, however, there are objects that do not exist, but about which true statements may nevertheless be made. In Meinong's terms, these objects *subsist*. Take Pegasus, for example, the flying horse from Greek lore. Meinong would say that although Pegasus does not exist, the sentence 'Pegasus flies' is true because somewhere out there, not in the same place as the existing things, but in some other place with the subsisting things, a certain horse is flying. Russell thought this was a terribly obscure view and one that we should be extremely reluctant to accept. Although Russell doesn't provide a very detailed argument against Meinong, it's clear there's a degree of strangeness here.[2]

The other way of explaining how 'the king of France' can have a meaning even if there is no king of France that Russell looks at is – surprise, surprise! – Frege's. You will remember that Frege's theory of names, which is also his theory of descriptions, involved a distinction between two kinds of meaning, sense and reference. One way to hold onto the idea that a description that refers to nothing can nevertheless be meaningful would be to say that it has a sense, but no reference. In fact, Frege often says exactly this, dedicating substantial attention to names like 'Pegasus' and 'Odysseus' and descriptions like 'the least rapidly converging series' and 'the celestial body furthest from Earth'.

At first glance, then, it might seem like Frege has an easy solution to the problem of empty names and descriptions. If we scratch a bit deeper, however, we can see that this response leads to a new problem. When we introduced Fregean senses earlier, we focused on two ways of characterizing them, as the mode of presentation of an object, and as the way the reference of an expression is determined. But the first characterization, at least, seems strained in the case of empty descriptions – how, you might wonder, can we have a mode of presentation if there is no object to be presented?

Although Frege's theory provides resources we might use to dissipate this mystery in various ways, philosophers to this day disagree both about which of those ways Frege himself meant to take, and about how successful they are. One way to go might be to say that we should rely less on the 'mode of presentation' metaphor from earlier, and more on some of the other ways of understanding what senses are. If we go back to our thought that senses are like directions or recipes, for example, it seems less obvious that we really need a referent. Think of directions that tell you how to find a buried treasure – we can still follow the directions, even if there turns out to be no treasure (maybe someone else has already taken it, maybe it was never there to begin with). It's a common theme in fantasy stories that some child will be born with a mark that indicates they're the chosen one. The evil emperor sends their minions out to all the villages every year to search for the child. When we read these stories, it seems like we understand perfectly well the sense in which the minions are looking for a particular thing, even if it doesn't exist (yet, or indeed, ever.)

Alternatively, we might hold onto the idea that senses involve a particular thing's being presented in a certain way, but loosen up our thinking about what kinds of things are presented by names and descriptions. In other words, we might look for something that could serve as the referent for an 'empty' name, without going full-on Meinong. Ordinarily, we take names and descriptions to present people and places. But we clearly have expressions in our language that refer to less concrete things, too, like numbers and relations, and some philosophers have thought that the sense of names like 'Pegasus' or descriptions like 'the least rapidly converging series' might be a mode of presentation of some of these. One idea that comes up in some of Frege's work is that 'empty' descriptions might really refer to the null set, the mathematical object that has no members. Other philosophers think that Frege's idea was that expressions like these actually have the thing we would expect to be their sense *as* their referent – Frege relies on a move like this when he talks about the reference of names that occur in certain indirect contexts, like in quotation or when we say things like 'Meinong believed that the least rapidly converging series was hard to find'. (You can learn more about this by looking at some of the readings I mention at the end of the chapter.)

To properly investigate the questions raised by these moves would take much more space than we have here. For us, what is important is that Russell didn't think any of them were any good. If empty descriptions have no reference, sentences involving them won't be true or false – Frege's view is that the truth value of a sentence like 'Pegasus flies' is determined by seeing whether the object referred to by 'Pegasus' has the property associated with the word 'flies'. But here there is no such object.

On the other hand, if empty descriptions have senses or the empty set as their referents, other strange consequences follow. Russell thinks it is clear, for example, that when we say things like 'The king of France is bald', we are talking about the world, not about the sense of the words 'the king of France'. Baldness is a property that people can have or not have, but which does not seem to apply to Fregean senses – we wouldn't, for example, say 'The sense of the description 'the king of France' is bald', anymore than we would 'the number 7 is bald'. This suggests that we either have to say that the meaning of the expression 'is bald' as it occurs in 'the king of England is bald' is different from the meaning of what looks to be the same word when it's used in 'the king of France is bald' – one picking out a property that applies to people, one a property that applies to senses – or say that whatever the meaning of 'bald' is, it can apply to people and senses. Similar reasoning would apply to the empty set hypothesis.

Russell has a strategy that he thinks allows us to avoid all of this oddness. The strategy depends on the claim that descriptions, despite appearances, don't really refer to anything in the first place. While Russell thinks it's in virtue of the way things are with Charles III that sentences involving the words 'the king of England' turn out true or false, he doesn't think the expression 'the king of England' *refers* to Charles, or to anyone else. So what is the relationship between the description and the guy?

Russell's theory depends on some technical machinery from logic that Frege played a key role in developing. That machinery involves the idea of **quantification**, which is, roughly, the idea that we can talk about how many objects have a certain property without actually naming or referring to them. Consider the following sentences, for example:

(12)   Everyone swims.

(13)   There is at least one person who swims.

(14)   There is at most one person who swims.

These sentences clearly have truth conditions – it's not hard to think of worlds that would make them false and worlds that would make them true. Any world in which there's any person who fails to swim makes (12) false. If there's anyone in a world who swims, (13) is true at that world, and if there are two different people in a world who swim, (14) is at that world. Crucially, however, and in contrast to proper names and even what might seem to be obviously the case with descriptions, the conditions expressed by (12)–(14) do nothing at all to specify *who* these people are. So it could be Arden who makes (13) true, or Jisoo, or both of them, or anyone else. The same goes for (12) and (14). If Jisoo fails to swim, (12) will be false, but since Zelenskyy has the same power to make the sentence true or false, the condition seems to apply just as much to him, and to Zaluzhnyi, and to everyone else. Quantificational sentences, then, put conditions on worlds without specifying anything about who the people who either meet or fail to meet those conditions are.

Russell's brilliant innovation with the theory of descriptions was to claim that definite descriptions, which on the face of things look like they're about a specific person, are in fact not. At the level of their true logical structure, Russell thinks, they really involve the conjunction of a group of quantificational claims. Specifically, when you say 'the *F* is *G*', for Russell you are saying:

Existence: There is at least one thing that is *F*.

Uniqueness: There is at most one thing that is *F*.

Predication: Everything that is *F* is *G*.

To apply this template to our examples involving the kings of England and France, Russell has it that those sentences are just shorthand ways of saying:

(15)   There is at least one king of England, and at most one king of England, and anything that is king of England is bald.

(16)   There is at least one king of France, and at most one king of France, and anything that is king of France is bald.

Is (15) true at the actual world? Well, to check, we have to check to see whether the conditions set out in its three clauses are met. Is there at least one king of England? Charles III has the property of being king of England, so the first condition is met. How about the second condition? There is no one aside from Charles who is king of England, so the second condition is met, too. What about the third condition? Is it the case that everything that is king of England is bald? Well, there's only one thing that's king of England, and it's bald, so this condition is met as well, and the sentence is true.

Now let's do (16). Is there at least one king of France? The answer here is clearly 'no', since France is a constitutional republic. This means the sentence is false, and we don't have to look at the other conditions.

Russell thinks these are exactly the intuitions that we should have about the sentences 'the king of England is bald' and 'the king of France is bald'. (If you have other intuitions about the king of France, we'll look at a different way you might handle sentences about him later on, in Chapter Four.) But his theory has an advantage over competitors that might produce the same result. To see that advantage, consider this sentence:

(17)   The king of France does not exist.

This sentence does indeed seem like a challenge for the theories we've looked at so far. If the expression 'the king of France' picks out a concrete individual, and then asserts of that individual that he doesn't exist, something confusing seems to have happened. On the other hand, if the description 'the king of France' picks out the empty set, it seems to falsely assert that that set doesn't exist, not to make the claim that there is no person who satisfies the description 'is king of France', as we'd intuitively expect.

But, on the other hand, an account based on Russell's three conditions has no difficulty making the natural prediction here. Russell's account says that when you utter (17) what you're saying is that it is false that there is an object that satisfies his conditions. If there is no king of France, then it *is* false that there is at least one king of France, and at most one king of France, which makes (17) true.

Many, perhaps even most philosophers to this day endorse versions of Russell's analysis of definite descriptions, and in general his technique of using tools from logic to explain away problems in the philosophy of language has been extremely influential.

NOTES

1. While there are striking differences of opinion about the truth conditions of certain hard cases, there seems to be broad agreement about a quite wide range of data. The extent of such agreements or disagreements, of course, is something that can be experimentally investigated, and its effect on the conclusions made by philosophers debated openly.

2. For what it is worth, some philosophers today actually accept something sort of like Meinong's view and have developed logics that allow us to talk about objects from both an 'inner' and an 'outer' domain. On these logics, sentences like 'so-and-so exists' are only true when the object picked out by the expression 'so-and-so' is in the inner domain, but sentences like 'so-and-so is tall' can be made true by objects from the outer domain. I've provided a reference for further reading on this topic at the end of the chapter.

FURTHER READING

Key sources for the material presented in this chapter include:

- Gottlob Frege. "Sense and reference". In: *Philosophical Review* 3 (1948), pp. 209–230.
- Saul Kripke. *Naming and Necessity*. Harvard University Press, 1980.

- Bertrand Russell. "On denoting". In: *Mind* 14.56 (1905), pp. 479–493.

For readers who want to explore related topics in greater detail, I recommend:

- Cumming, Sam, "Names", The Stanford Encyclopedia of Philosophy (Winter 2023 Edition), Edward N. Zalta & Uri Nodelman (eds.),
- LaPorte, Joseph, "Rigid Designators", The Stanford Encyclopedia of Philosophy (Winter 2022 Edition), Edward N. Zalta & Uri Nodelman (eds.),
- Ludlow, Peter, "Descriptions", The Stanford Encyclopedia of Philosophy (Winter 2023 Edition), Edward N. Zalta & Uri Nodelman (eds.)
- Michaelson, Eliot, "Reference", The Stanford Encyclopedia of Philosophy (Summer 2024 Edition), Edward N. Zalta & Uri Nodelman (eds.)
- P.F. Strawson. "On referring". In: *Mind* 59.235 (1950), pp. 320–344.
- Stepen Read. *Thinking about Logic*. Oxford University Press, 1995.

METASEMANTICS

In Chapter Two, we looked at a number of philosophical disputes involving semantics, that is, disputes involving questions about what certain words (or groups of words) mean. We saw, for example, how Frege took identity statements like 'Hesperus is Phosphorus' to show that there must be more to the meaning of a name than the object named. And we saw how Kripke took our intuition that statements like 'Aristotle taught Alexander the Great' are neither necessary nor analytic to show that the property of having taught Alexander can't fix the reference or be part of the meaning of the name 'Aristotle'. Although we didn't try to give a definitive resolution of this tension – spoiler alert: such resolutions will not often occur in philosophy! – I hope that by looking closely at it you will have gotten a sense of how discussion in one of the major research areas of the philosophy of language is conducted.

In this chapter we will turn our attention to another area of the philosophy of language. Here, again, our goal will not be to attempt to survey all of the work that's been done in that area, but rather to use discussion of a few key topics to provide a sense of how the game is played, and thus a foundation for further study.

The area we will focus on in this chapter is called **metasemantics**. As you may guess from the name, metasemantics involves questions

DOI: 10.4324/9781003250753-3

that are posed at a greater level of generality than semantic questions are. When doing metasemantics, philosophers are trying to figure out not what the meaning of a certain expression is, but *how* the expression comes to have that meaning. While I can imagine some philosophers arguing that they will ultimately come to the same thing, I think it will be helpful as we get started to distinguish between two sorts of metasemantic projects. On the one hand, we have what we might call questions about **narrow metasemantics**: here, we might ask why the name 'John F. Kennedy' refers to John F. Kennedy instead of referring to some other object or nothing at all. On the other hand, we have what I'll call **broad metasemantic** questions, like 'what makes a series of sounds/signs meaningful in the first place'?

We'll begin the chapter by looking at two narrow metasemantic theories – theories that assume a Millian semantics for names and aim to explain how a particular object comes to be the referent of a particular name. Then we'll turn to a pair of broad metasemantic theories – theories that aim to explain where linguistic meanings come from.

3.1 PROPER NAMES

3.1.1 KRIPKE'S CAUSAL/HISTORICAL METASEMANTICS

As we have just said, to give a narrow metasemantic theory about a certain kind of expression is to give a theory that aims to explain why instances of that kind of expression have the particular meanings they do. To give a narrow metasemantic theory of names, then, is to give a theory that aims to explain not *what* names mean, but *how* they come to have those meanings.

Take the Fregean theory we considered in Chapter Two, for example, according to which names have a kind of hybrid meaning that involves both a referent and a sense. Suppose, for the sake of argument, that we accept this view and agree that the meaning of 'Socrates' is a complex involving a certain person and a certain mode of presentation of that person – a mode that involves his being the teacher of Alexander the Great, say. Can you see that accepting this much would leave room open for us to wonder what makes it the case that *this* mode of presentation is the one associated with that name, instead of some other mode of presentation, or nothing at all? This is the space in which metasemantic debates take place.

Although Frege doesn't talk in terms of semantics/metasemantics, many of the things he says do suggest a particular take on what we would nowadays think of as metasemantic questions. Consider his remarks about how different people are likely to associate different senses with the name 'Aristotle', for example. As we saw in Chapter Two, for one person the sense of the name 'Aristotle' might involve the property of having been a student of Plato, while for another the sense of the name involves the property of having been the teacher of Alexander the Great.

What, we might ask, makes it the case that for the first person, the name 'Aristotle' has one of these senses, while for the second person, it has the other sense? Frege's remarks suggest that the answer involves something that happens in each person's mind. When the first person thinks of, hears, or uses the name, somehow the property of someone's being a student of Plato is mentally activated for them, and when the second person thinks of, hears, or uses the name, the property of someone's being a teacher of Alexander is mentally activated for them.

Since Frege's official claim is that the meaning of a name is a hybrid involving both a sense and a reference, what I am about to say is not strictly speaking right. But if we pretend for a moment that the meaning of a name is *only* its referent, while retaining the idea that sense determines reference, we can think of senses themselves as performing a kind of metasemantic work. Senses, remember, specify which object a name picks out. On the Fregean picture, as well as on the forms of descriptivism Kripke argued against, senses do this job by imposing certain conditions that must be met in order for an object to count as the referent of a word.

Views like this make the relationship between names and their referents a relationship based on what philosophers sometimes call **satisfaction**. An object comes to count as the referent of an expression in virtue of its **satisfying** some conditions the expression imposes. We can think of satisfaction by analogy with the children's toy that is made of a box with different-shaped holes cut into the lid. If the toy is well made, just one block will fit in each hole; so the star-shaped block fits only in the star-shaped hole, the triangle-shaped block fits only in the triangle-shaped hole, and so on. Senses would be like extremely fine-grained holes, shaped so precisely that just one object would fit into them – finding the referent of an expression would be like going around the world, holding the sense up to every object to see 'Will this fit? Will this?', until you find the one object that does.

The reason I mention this, even though it isn't quite right that Frege's theory of senses was a metasemantic theory (given that he thinks senses are a part of meaning), is that it points the way toward a problem Kripke acknowledges at the beginning of his lectures. Despite all the issues he points out for the descriptive theory, Kripke takes care to emphasize that one thing descriptivism does well is explain how certain words come to be hooked up with certain things in the world – by means of the satisfaction relation. If we get rid of senses, we lose this satisfaction story, which means we have to go and find a new one. Since Kripke thinks all there is to the meaning of a name is the thing named, he needs to come up with a story that explains how names get attached to their referents.

The story he tells – which he takes care to avoid calling a theory – is one that he calls the 'causal/historical' picture of names. Here is how he introduces it:

> Someone, let's say, a baby, is born; his parents call him by a certain name. They talk about him to their friends. Other people meet him. Through various sorts of talk the name is spread from link to link as if by a chain. A speaker who is on the far end of this chain, who has heard about, say, Richard Feynman, in the marketplace or elsewhere, may be referring to Richard Feynman even though he can't remember from whom he first heard of Feynman or from whom he ever heard of Feynman.
> (Kripke 1980, 91)

The picture has two key components, which Kripke blends together a bit in this passage. One component involves the way new names are introduced into a language for the first time – Kripke calls this an **initial baptism** – and the other component involves the way names are transmitted from person to person once they have been introduced.

Typically, initial baptisms will involve speakers who are in direct perceptual contact with the objects they introduce names for. When parents decide that the baby they are looking at or holding will be called 'Richard Feynman', they are stipulating that that name will apply to the baby they are holding. The fact that looking at or holding are *causal* relations is crucial here – if a mix-up in the hospital meant that the baby Feynman's parents were holding when they said 'this baby shall henceforth be known as "Richard Feynman"' turned out not to be theirs, the fact that they thought the baby was theirs wouldn't change anything about the fact that the name applies to what it does: the baby they were holding.

Once Feynman's parents have given him his name, the name can be passed on to other people who can then come to use it to pick him out. Suppose, for example, that a bit later on Feynman's birthday, one of his parents goes to the hospital office to file some paperwork concerning the baby. Someone in the office asks 'what is your baby's name?' and the parent says 'Richard'. Now the office person asks 'how much did Richard weigh when he was born?' It seems clear that this question refers to baby Feynman, that is, to the baby the parents performed an initial baptism on. But the clerk in the office has never seen that baby. In virtue of what is it the case that when they say 'Richard' they refer to the baby?

Here again causation has a key role to play. Think about why the clerk used the word 'Richard' when they wanted to ask about the baby born to the parent standing in front of them. They use that term because the parent used it – if the parents had initially baptized Richard with the name Woobin the clerk would have said Woobin and so on. In other words, there is a causal dependence here, with its roots in a certain name-giving event, an event which itself involved a certain baby.

The same structure of causal dependence that connects the clerk – through Feynman's parents – to Feynman can be extended from person to person in a broad community, making it possible for everyone to use a name to refer to a certain individual, even if most members have had no independent contact with the baby. If at some later point someone in the paperwork-filing department notices that there is a blank space on the form the clerk filled in, they might say to a colleague 'Oh no, someone forgot to fill in Richard Feynman's weight.

How will we ever find that information now?' Intuitively, this statement would clearly be a statement about Feynman. On Kripke's picture, that aboutness is explained by the fact that it is the initial baptism of Feynman that lies at the end of the causal chain that led to the use of the expression 'Richard Feynman'.

This basic structure can be applied to very long chains, involving objects that are very far from us in time and space, and about which we would never be able to provide a uniquely individuating description. Think again about Einstein or Aristotle. The fact that the only description someone could give of Albert Einstein would involve saying that he invented the atomic bomb is immaterial on Kripke's story – a person who says such a thing, for Kripke, is saying it about Einstein, in virtue of the fact that they got the name 'Albert Einstein' from someone who got it from someone who got it from … someone who used it to baptize Albert Einstein.

The same is true of us when we talk about Aristotle. In fact, this is a particularly important case to consider because it is very unlikely that the name Aristotle's parents gave him looked or sounded anything like the name we use today – no initial baptism that Aristotle's parents would have performed would have involved sounds very much like the ones we make in English today. Nevertheless, Kripke's story presumes that there is an unbroken causal chain that relates our uses of the expression 'Aristotle' to a particular person, who is the person we talk about when we use that name. At the beginning of the chain there will be an initial baptism, presumably one performed by Aristotle's parents. That baptism will have resulted in a practice of using some name to refer to Aristotle, which spreads throughout a population and over time by the mechanism described here so far. Then at some point, the name 'jumps' from one language to another, or from one dialect to another. How could this work?

One idea would be to treat the new name as though it involved another kind of baptism – people speaking one language might decide, say, that Aristotle's name in Greek was too hard to pronounce and so they introduce a new term with the stipulation that it refers to whatever Aristotle's name in Greek referred to. Alternatively, it might happen that the speakers of the mutated version of the name take themselves to be saying it the same way speakers of the original name said it. As long as they make whatever sound they do with the intention of preserving the original practice, Kripke can say that they are in a sense preserving that practice. After all, the sounds they are making are sounds they are making because of the fact that people they met made the sounds they did, which trace back to Aristotle's parents making some sounds.

Thinking about the way in which a name can mutate or even undergo a step-change over time while still being causally related to the same object as the original name brings out an important point of clarification that needs to be made about causal chains and the transmission of names. Kripke does not think that *any* causal chain relating your uses of a certain sound to a certain object means that the sound picks out the object. Suppose, to take an example of his, that you hear someone talking about Napoleon and think 'That would be a lovely name for my aardvark', and then you start calling your aardvark 'Napoleon'. In this case, there is a causal chain linking your uses of the name 'Napoleon' to the French emperor – you wouldn't be pronouncing 'Napoleon' in front of your pet if Napoleon's name hadn't been what it was. But in this case when you hear people talking about Napoleon you don't have the intention to be using the name in the same way as they do. Kripke's causal/historical model depends, then, not just on causal links but on causal links that go together with an *intention* to participate in the same practice.

3.1.2 INTERLUDE: SEMANTIC EXTERNALISM – NAMES FOR 'STUFF'?

Before moving on to consider an alternative narrow metasemantics for names, I'd like to briefly call attention to some ways in which our discussion of the questions Kripke's view raises parallel discussions about a class of expressions that includes more than just names for individuals. The expressions I have in mind are often called **natural kind terms** by philosophers; we might think of them as names, not for individual objects, but for *types* of objects. Prominent examples from the literature include physical types like 'water', 'jade', and 'gold', as well as biological types like 'tiger'.

In the literature on natural kinds, descriptivist-style and causal-style views are often referred to as **semantic internalism** and **semantic externalism**. Very roughly, the difference between the views consists in how they answer the question 'Do the facts about what our words mean depend on facts about the world outside our minds?' Simplifying somewhat, the internalist says 'no' and the externalist says 'yes'.

Frege's view is a bit tricky because he thinks of meaning as a complex involving sense and reference. But a caricatured version of descriptivism can help to bring out the difference between the two camps. Suppose we have Kripke's causal/historical metasemantics for names on one hand, and a view that says that the meaning of a name is equivalent to the meaning of a definite description, on the other. So, one theory says the meaning of the name 'John F. Kennedy' is a certain person (Kennedy himself), and the other says the name means the same thing as, say, the description 'the 35th president of the United States'.

Here, the Kripke-style theory is *externalist* and the descriptivist theory *internalist* in the following sense: if the world outside of you is different from the way you think it is, and the Kripke theory is true, your name 'John F. Kennedy' might have a different meaning from the meaning you think it has. If descriptivism is true, on the other hand, there's a sense in which changes in the world would have no effect on the meaning of your expression. If you associate the description 'the 35th president of the United States' with the name 'John F. Kennedy', then although changes in the world might mean that different people are satisfied with that description, the meaning of your name remains constant.

Hilary Putnam, another leading figure from 20th-century philosophy, offered a famous thought experiment designed to highlight intuitions that support externalism about natural kind terms. Putnam's experiment goes like this. Not in another metaphysically possible world, but in a distant corner of our own galaxy, there is a star exactly like our sun, orbited by however many planets and asteroids orbit our sun, all with exactly the shape of the planets and asteroids we are familiar with. On the third planet out from that sun – which Putnam calls 'Twin Earth' – everything looks exactly the way it does here. In fact, pretty much everything *is* exactly the way it is here. There's a house just like my house, and a house just like yours, and in each of them lives a person that looks just like each of us, responds to the same name, and so on. Twin Earth is an atom-for-atom duplicate of Earth, except for one difference: instead of H_2O, the liquid that fills the rivers and streams on Twin Earth is composed of a substance with a very different chemical composition that in our discussion here we will abbreviate as 'XYZ'.

Now suppose you are writing a grant proposal and you are interested in the question of how much water there is in the galaxy. You write on your proposal 'I hypothesize that there are n^m grams of water in the galaxy', where n and m are some very large numbers. Your twin on Twin Earth, of course, is also writing a grant proposal and writes something that looks like exactly the same sentence. Do your sentences mean the same thing? Suppose the amounts of H_2O and XYZ in the galaxy are not the same. In such a case, would one of your sentences be wrong?

Putnam thinks that when you use the word 'water' and when your twin uses their word that looks and sounds just like our word, you are talking about different things. When you say 'water', you're talking about H_2O, and when your twin uses their twin-word, they're talking about XYZ. So if you have both written the same number of grams on the page, only one of you (if either) can be right.

Why is this? Putnam's answer is that your (our) word 'water' picks out H_2O because that is the substance we have causal contact with. Your twin's word – which just happens to look and sound like our word 'water' – picks out XYZ because that is the substance your twin, and members of your twin's society, have causal contact with. Although Putnam doesn't imagine there was ever anything like the kind of initial baptism Kripke thought could be found at the end of the causal chain of uses of a name, his idea is similar in that it treats the reference of natural kind terms as being fixed by a kind of pointing at the environment. Instead of it being the case that any stuff that is colorless, odorless, and drinkable counts as water, then, the idea is that only stuff which is microphysically similar to *this stuff right here* (uttered by someone holding some H_2O) is water.

Putnam's view counts as externalism by our rough-and-ready characterization because it makes the reference of 'water' depend not just on how things our with our minds, but on how things are out in the world. If the colorless, odorless, drinkable stuff filling the lakes and streams around here had been some other chemical instead of H_2O, our uses of the term 'water' would have picked out that stuff instead.

3.1.3 EVANS' RESPONSE TO THE 'MADAGASCAR' PROBLEM

Now let's turn our attention back to proper names. As influential as Kripke's metasemantics for names has been, it is not the only non-descriptive picture in town. Before we turn our attention to what I earlier called 'broad' metasemantic questions, I'd like to introduce an alternative to Kripke's picture that provides another possible way of explaining – without relying on the notion of satisfaction – how a name might come to be linked with the object it names.

Gareth Evans brought the interesting history of the name 'Madagascar' to Kripke's attention and claimed that it caused serious problems for his causal/historical picture. Evans presents the case as follows:

> We learn from Isaac Taylor's book: *Names and their History*, 1898: 'In the case of "Madagascar" a hearsay report of Malay or Arab sailors misunderstood by Marco Polo has had the effect of transferring a corrupt form of the name of a portion of the African mainland to the great African Island'.
> (Evans 1973, 195)

In other words, something that sounded sort of like our word 'Madagascar' was used by people living on the east coast of Africa as a name for some part of Africa (some people think Somalia, from 'Mogadishu'). Sailors heard them talking about that place using that word and adopted it themselves, and then when Marco Polo asked them questions about the geography of the region they used it in their reply. He formed the impression that the sailors were talking about an island, which led him to write things like 'Madagascar is a very large island off the coast of Africa' in a book, which many people later read, bringing the name 'Madagascar' into wide circulation.

The problem here for Kripke is that at each step in this process, the people who acquired the expression 'Madagascar' meant to be using it in a way that was consistent with the people from whom they acquired it. So when the sailors say 'Madagascar', they intended to be talking about the same place as the local people they heard speaking. When Marco Polo wrote the term down, he took himself to be doing the same. When Marco Polo's readers started using the expression 'Madagascar', they meant to be talking about whatever he was. And so on, all the way down to the present day. By Kripke's lights, this should mean that when we say 'Madagascar', we are talking about a portion of the African mainland – that, after all, is the object that lies at the end of the relevant causal chains. But when we use the name 'Madagascar', we are clearly talking about the big island off the east coast of Africa!

Evans has an ingenious solution to this problem. That solution depends on the idea that each of us has, corresponding to each name we are familiar with, a dossier or 'mental file' of information purporting to relate to that name. When we first hear a new name, we open a new dossier, labeling it with that name, and as we hear the name used, we add information to the dossier.

Suppose, for example, that you're at a party and you hear people talking about someone called 'Kit'. You hear things like 'Ah, Kit is so smart! I heard they invented the zipper. Could that be true? It wouldn't surprise me, I mean, they did go to a really good engineering school.' If you think the person being talked about is a person you've never heard of before, you open a new mental file and label it 'Kit'. In the file you put the information you have about the person in question – in this case, that they may have invented the zipper, that they're really smart (or that the person speaking thought so), and that they went to a really good engineering school. Whenever you hear more statements made about Kit, you add more information to the file.

So far this might remind you of the cluster theory version of descriptivism – the cluster theorist, remember, said that names are associated with a cluster of descriptions and that the object the name refers to is the object that satisfies a majority of the descriptions, or the most important ones, or whatever. But Evans is no descriptivist. The genius of his theory is to say that the object that is picked out by a name is not the object that *satisfies* most of the descriptions in the dossier, but the object that is *causally responsible* for most of the descriptions' being in the dossier in the first place.

Suppose, to elaborate more on our 'Kit' case, that it turns out that there is a certain person who goes around pretending to have invented the zipper and to have gone to a really good engineering school. Suppose that person didn't do any of the things commonly attributed to them, but that they are charismatic and a bit of a trickster, and that they have made many people think they did many interesting things.

If the trickster is causally responsible for people's grouping descriptions like 'invented the zipper' and 'went to a really good engineering school together under the heading 'Kit', they are the referent of that name, whether they were ever baptized with it or not. In a case like this, your Kit file would be a file that contains information that doesn't really apply to Kit, in the sense of being true of, but which 'points to' Kit in the sense of being *caused* by Kit. If Kit hadn't existed you wouldn't have created that file. If Kit hadn't done the things they'd done, your file wouldn't look the way it does, and so on.

One important thing to notice about Evans' story is that over time, the proportion of information in a dossier that is due to one or another object can change. Think of the Dread Pirate Roberts from the film *The Princess Bride*. (Spoiler alert!) In that film, it turns out that what people thought for many years was a single, terrifying pirate, was in fact a series of different pirates, each training a successor when it was time for them to retire.

Imagine that in such a scenario, the first Dread Pirate Roberts spent only a little time marauding and was happy to retire early and spend most of his time growing cucumbers. He hands off the ship and the costume to a new pirate. At this stage, when the people of coastal towns tell stories to their kids about the Dread Pirate Roberts, they're clearly talking about Pirate 1 – he's the one who is responsible for everyone's Dread Pirate Roberts files. But then Pirate 2 comes along and does a lot of really crazy stuff. No one knows about the handoff, so they keep a single Dread Pirate Roberts file, but over time, the exploits associated with the name 'Dread Pirate Roberts' come to be dominated by things Pirate 2 did or which Pirate 2's doings led to. At this point, intuitively, it seems like the name 'Dread Pirate Roberts' should refer to Pirate 2. This is exactly the result Evans' story predicts.

While it's clear that a lot of work would have to be done to turn this little sketch into a theory – which descriptions are the important ones, how many have to be causally due to a certain person in order for that person to count as the referent of a name, what happens with mixed files, merged files, etc., files about nothing, etc. – I hope there is enough here to give you a sense of how a theory might go, and how it would help with our Madagascar problem.

> Can you reconstruct Evans' explanation of why our word 'Madagascar' picks out the island, and not the mainland?

3.2   THE ORIGIN OF MEANING

3.2.1   GRICE'S INTENTION-BASED THEORY

Now that we've had a chance to look at some metasemantic questions as they arise in connection with names, I'd like to take a step back and look at some of the responses philosophers have given to the more general question of where linguistic meanings come from in the first place.

In order to set the stage for that discussion, let me call attention to a point that might have occurred to you while thinking about Kripke's and Evans' metasemantic theories: although those theories look promising when applied to names for individuals and maybe for kinds, it isn't easy to see how they could be extended in a general way to cover all of language. Causal connections between ourselves and the things we talk about are at the heart of both theories – but it seems like many of the words we use don't involve causal relationships, or indeed, a connection to objects at all.

Words like 'beauty' and 'truth', for example, clearly have meanings, but it isn't clear that they involve objects or events that we could be in causal contact with. The same is true for mathematical language, for logic, and so on; it seems pretty clear that words like 'and' and 'or' have meanings – if they didn't, what would explain our intuition that they mean different things? – but it seems unlikely that we have causal contact with an object that they pick out. It seems even less likely that someone performed an initial baptism involving 'or' – what could they be baptizing? – or that each of us maintains a dossier such that whichever object was causally responsible for most of the descriptions in it is the one 'and' picks out. Even if we like the Kripke or the Evans metasemantics for names, then, it seems clear that it will at most get us part of the way toward explaining where linguistic meanings come from.

Paul Grice, a British philosopher working in the second half of the 20th century, developed a very influential theory that aimed to give a general analysis of linguistic meaning. To put things very simply, the heart of Grice's theory is the idea that the things we say have meanings because we *intend* them to and that they have the particular meanings they do because we intend for them to have those meanings. (This approach raises questions here about how our thoughts get meanings, but those are questions for another day).

To see how Grice's theory works, think for a moment about the variety of ways in which we ordinarily say things like '*x* means *y*'. In English – and in many other languages besides – we often use variations on this formula where nothing remotely linguistic seems to be at stake:

(18)   Those spots mean measles.

(19)   The recent snowfall means we're going to have to find another road.

Grice calls the kind of meaning that is at issue in these examples **natural meaning**, and he points out several characteristic features. The most important of these is that when we say '*x* means *y*' in the sense of natural meaning, we take *x* to entail *y*. So you can't say 'although those spots mean measles, the patient doesn't have measles' or 'the snowfall means we'll have to find another road, but we won't, this one will be fine'. To put this in terms of our previous discussion of tree rings and tracks in the snow from Chapter One, we might say that natural meaning involves one thing's being a non-arbitrary sign of another.

When we were looking for a working definition of language in Chapter One, we saw some reasons for thinking that arbitrariness was an important property. Grice's theory involves a similar idea. At the root of language, he thinks, lies something he calls **non-natural meaning**, which he abbreviates by writing 'meaning$_{NN}$' and illustrates with examples like the following:

(20)   Those three rings on the bell (of the bus) mean that the bus is full.

(21)   That red flag with the white slash means there are divers around the boat.

Unlike in the case of examples (18) and (19), there's nothing strange about following these sentences up with a negation. So, you might say 'Although those three rings of the bell mean the bus is full, it isn't! Look at all that space! I guess the driver is trying to keep the schedule.' Grice takes this gap between a sign and what it means to be one of the hallmarks of language, and he offers several strategies for defining meaning$_{NN}$ before setting on one that he thinks does the trick. Since each of his preliminary attempts brings out important features of the terrain, it will be worth taking a look even at the views he doesn't think end up succeeding.

The first view is one that Grice calls the **causal/correlative account**:

> For x to mean$_{NN}$ something, x must have (roughly) a tendency to produce in an audience some attitude (cognitive or otherwise) and a tendency, in the case of a speaker, to be produced by that attitude, these tendencies being dependent on an elaborate process of conditioning attending the use of the sign in communication.
> (Grice 1957, 379)

There are clear problems with the causal/correlative definition of meaning$_{NN}$. Consider what happens when I put on a tailcoat. It is plausible to think that this is in fact the kind of thing that will cause you to believe that I am going to a dance. Who would put on a tailcoat if they weren't going to a dance? Because tailcoat-donning does tend to produce the belief that someone is going to a dance, it meets the first condition from the definition. It also meets the second condition, since tailcoat-donning is also the kind of thing that will normally be caused by someone's believing that they're going to a dance. Nevertheless, Grice thinks it's clear that my putting on a tailcoat doesn't mean$_{NN}$ that I'm going to a dance. It sounds weird to say 'his putting on a tailcoat means he's going to a dance, but he isn't going to a dance'. Even if the relationship between tailcoat-donnings and going to dances is less regular than the relation between, say, tree rings and a tree's age, it doesn't seem to involve enough arbitrariness to count as properly linguistic.

Grice proposes improving on the causal/correlative account by getting speakers' intentions into the game. As a first attempt at doing that, he offers the following:

Intentions:
x means$_{NN}$ that P just in case x is intended by its utterer to induce in an audience the belief that P.

But problems arise quickly for this first intention-based account, too. Suppose you want the police to believe that your roommate committed a murder. You leave your roommate's handkerchief at the scene of the crime, knowing that if they find it, they'll conclude that the culprit was your roommate. Grice thinks it is clear that while you might succeed this way in causing the police to form a certain belief, your leaving the handkerchief is not a case of meaning$_{NN}$ – among other things, it seems like it would be odd in such a case for someone in the know to say 'the handkerchief means that so-and-so is the murderer'.

Part of the issue here is that when the police encounter the handkerchief, they take it simply as evidence – as a non-arbitrary sign. While your intentions that the police form a certain belief might have been what drove you to leave it, if those intentions were visible to the police, your trick wouldn't have worked. Considerations like this lead Grice to a reformulation:

Transparent intentions
x means$_{NN}$ that P just in case x is intended by its utterer to induce in an audience the belief that P and this intention is recognized by the audience.

This attempt, too, however, seems to fall short. Remember our discussion from Chapter One about the head of John the Baptist? Grice's paper 'Meaning' is the place where that example comes into the philosophy of language. While discussing the example, Grice points out that by presenting Salome with the severed head, Herod intends to induce the belief in her that John is dead. It seems pretty clear his action will succeed in producing that belief. It also seems clear that his intention will be recognized – Salome is not likely to wonder why Herod is bringing her a severed head. Since she'll form the belief and recognize Herod's intention that she form it, the foregoing definition entails that the head-presentation means$_{NN}$ that John is dead.

But our Chapter One discussion made clear, it doesn't seem like the sense in which you get someone to believe that a person is dead by displaying a severed head is the same sense as the sense in which you get them to believe something when you use language to communicate that information. There (in terms influenced by Grice, in fact), we put things in terms of a difference between *showing* and *telling*. Even if you show someone something in a way that makes it clear that you mean to be showing them something, that is, in which your intention that they learn something new is obvious, there's a sense in which it's the object shown that does the work in causing their belief to be formed.

In order to capture what is really distinctive about the kind of thing that happens when you *tell* someone something instead of showing them, Grice thinks we need to build into our definition the requirement that your audience not only recognize your intention, but that their recognition of that intention *plays a significant role* in explaining why they form the new belief they do. To make this point, he asks us to consider the difference between two ways I might aim to influence your beliefs. Adapting an example of his, consider the following cases:

(22) I show you a photograph of your roommate stealing and eating your Cheetos.

(23) I show you a sketch I have drawn of your roommate stealing and eating your Cheetos.

Suppose in each of these scenarios, my showing you what I show you leads you to form the belief that your roommate is stealing your Cheetos. In both cases, moreover, you see that I intend you to form that belief. Only in the second case, however, does your recognition of my intention have any explanatory work to play. Where the photograph is concerned, your engagement with my intentions is beside the point – you would form the belief in question whether I'd anonymously left the photo in your office, or in your car, or whatever. When I sketch the theft for you, on the other hand, it isn't the lines on the page *themselves* that do the work making you think that the roommate is the thief, it's your recognition that I am trying to get you to think as much. If you don't recognize that intention – if you just take me to be exploring my creativity, or trying to amuse you, or whatever – you won't form the belief.

This leads us, finally, to a formulation Grice thinks in fact captures the intuitions we began with:

> Reflexive intentions:
> x means$_{NN}$ that P just in case x is intended by its utterer to induce in an audience the belief that P by means of the recognition of this intention.

The kind of intentions at stake in this definition are sometimes called **reflexive**, because of the fact that they point back at themselves in a certain way. It isn't enough, as we've seen, for you to intend to get someone to think that P, or for you to intend that they see you intending them to think that P – the key to meaning$_{NN}$ for Grice is that their recognition of your intention be the thing that *leads* them to come to have the belief that P.

As a final illustration of the way in which reflexive intentions can cause changes in an audience's mental states, Grice points to the difference between getting a greedy person out of your office by dropping a banknote out the window and by pointing to the door. In the former case, the person's leaving is explained entirely by their seeing the money head toward the ground outside. But in the latter, it's their seeing *that I intend* for them to see that I want them to leave that causes them to leave. The same goes, Grice says, for cases in which a police officer stops a car by standing in front of it, as opposed to waving at the driver, and, in a fascinating extension of the basic structure of his theory of meaning$_{NN}$, cases in which I cut in front of you on the street. I may, Grice says, make you angry or frustrated simply by getting in front of you and slowing you down. But something distinctive happens if I do it in a way that involves a reflexive intention – if you see that I want you to see that I mean to insult you, you may, in addition to the simple frustration of having your path blocked, feel *insulted*.

Before considering some philosophical challenges Grice's theory raises, it will be worth calling attention to two points about his theory that might have occurred to you. The first concerns the nature of the intentions the theory is based on. You might think 'Wait a second, this sounds like a very complicated process. In order to tell you that your roommate is stealing your Cheetos, I have to produce a certain sound (writing, gesture, etc.) with the aim of getting you to see that by producing that sound I meant for you to form the belief that your roommate is stealing your Cheetos?! But that isn't an intention that it seems like I'm forming. In fact, it seems like our mental lives would be overpopulated by thoughts about thoughts, if this picture were true.'

Grice is careful to emphasize that he is sensitive to this kind of worry and that he does not take the intentions at stake here to be intentions that rise to the level of conscious deliberation. Grice, and people nowadays who endorse versions of his theory, will typically say that we have reflexive communicative intentions in something like the sense in which a person who opens a door intends to unclasp their thumb and forefinger to grab the door handle, or a person who shifts gears in a car intends to decouple the flywheel from the transmission by pushing in the clutch pedal – these aren't things we think about, but which nevertheless count as intentional.

The other point of clarification that deserves to be flagged concerns the precise nature of the question Grice's theory, as we have presented it here so far, actually answers. Recall that we started off this section with the very general question of how linguistic expressions end up with meanings. Hopefully our discussion of Grice will give you a sense of how his answer will go – it'll involve speakers' reflexive intentions, that is, their intention that their audience come to form certain beliefs (etc.) on the basis of their recognizing those intentions of speakers.

You may have noticed, however, that the definitions of meaning$_{NN}$ that we gave above all involve particular instances – the theory is focused on explaining what a particular person meant by some particular words on a particular occasion. Suppose Kit says to Char 'Your roommate is stealing your Cheetos'. Then we can ask metasemantic questions like: how does Kit's utterance come to have a meaning? How does it come to have the meaning it does? And now we have seen how to use Grice's theory to give answers: Grice will say that Kit's utterance has meaning because it was produced with the right kind of reflexive intention, and it has the meaning it does because of the specific nature of the reflexive intention with which it was produced – that is, the intention that the hearer form the belief that their roommate is stealing their Cheetos in virtue of recognizing that Kit intended them to form that belief.

But how, you might wonder, do we get from this to a story about what the sentence 'Your roommate is stealing your Cheetos' means$_{NN}$? Or to a story about what the word 'your' means, or the word 'stealing'? Grice and many philosophers who find his approach congenial tend to want to resist questions like this. Sometimes they offer a slogan: 'words don't mean things, people do'. They think that meaning is fundamentally something people do – in fact, the notion of meaning Grice develops is often called **speaker meaning** to highlight the primacy of the speaker in generating meanings – and that the sense in which sentences or words have a 'timeless' meaning, as Grice puts it, is a derivative one.

In Grice's article, he suggests that we might think of the meaning of a sentence or a word in terms of the set of occasions on which people have used it. On this picture, the meaning of the sentence 'Your roommate is stealing your Cheetos' would be the set of all the propositions people have reflexively intended their audiences to believe when producing that sentence. If we look at all of those propositions, we will presumably see a large degree of commonality – all of them will involve someone stealing, a roommate, some Cheetos, and so on. We might use a variation on this trick to approach the question of the 'dictionary' meaning of words, too. Consider the set of all of the beliefs people have ever intended others to form by using the word 'Cheetos'. Those beliefs will be dramatically diverse – they'll involve different places, times, agents, tastes, and so on. But there will presumably be a common thread running through them, a thread involving a crispy orange snack. This doesn't mean that the word 'Cheetos' means$_{NN}$ Cheetos – that wouldn't be a well-formed thing to say, as you can't believe Cheetos, and meaning$_{NN}$ is about intending that someone form a belief. But it can explain our lingering sense that the meaning of 'Cheetos' has something to do with a snack food.

Grice's theory has been tremendously influential, and there are philosophers even today who think that some version of it is right. As is the case with any philosophical theory, however, there are problems, too. We will consider two of those, and some responses, here.

The first problem can be brought out by considering a very famous passage from *Alice in Wonderland*, which philosophers love to quote when talking about meaning:

> 'I don't know what you mean by "glory"', Alice said.
> Humpty Dumpty smiled contemptuously. 'Of course you don't – till I tell you. I meant "there's a nice knock-down argument for you!"'

'But glory' doesn't mean "a nice knock-down argument"', Alice objected.
'When I use a word', Humpty Dumpty said, in rather a scornful tone, 'it
means just what I choose it to mean – neither more nor less'.
'The question is', said Alice, 'whether you can make words mean so many
different things'.
'The question is', said Humpty Dumpty, 'Which is to be master – that's all'.

This passage illustrates a tension between two natural thoughts. On
the one hand, we have good reasons for thinking that a speaker's
intentions are important when questions about meaning arise, and we
just have seen that these can be developed in a systematic way. On the
other hand, we have the sense that where questions of meaning are
concerned, it isn't the case that just anything goes. Although Humpty
Dumpty says that his words mean whatever he wants them to mean,
Alice disagrees.

Who do you think is right? Suppose you go to a restaurant and
say 'I'll have a steak, please', intending to order a grilled portobello
mushroom. What dish do you think you'll get? I suppose few of us
would expect to get a mushroom in a case like this. If someone who
said 'Steak please!' were to complain when the meat arrives, saying
'I said 'steak' but what I intended to convey was that I wanted a
portobello mushroom!' it does not seem likely that they would get
very far. This seems to be a fairly strong consideration in support of
Alice's side of her dispute with Humpty Dumpty.

One way for Grice to avoid this problem might be to point out
that it isn't really the case that you can just intend whatever you like.
Can you intend to jump over the moon? Can you intend to become
a cat? Of course, you might wish to jump over the moon or become
a cat, and you might try to jump as high as you can or take frequent naps curled up in the sun. But it seems like a stretch to think
that someone doing these things could really have intentions involving a trip past the moon or becoming a cat. This suggests that our
expectations about the likely outcomes of our actions have a role to
play in constraining what we can intend, and thus, on Grice's theory, what we can mean. If you know that saying 'I would like to
have a steak' will cause people to form the belief that you would like
to have a steak, then it seems hard to see how you could produce
that sentence with the intention that they form a belief involving a
portobello mushroom.

The idea that a speaker's reasonable expectations place constraints on the things they can use their words to mean is a popular one in philosophy. But it does involve some consequences that are worth pointing out. First of all, we might wonder: does this mean that if you're mistaken about how people will respond, you can mean really bizarre things? If you're under a temporary delusion, for example, that 'steak' means 'mushroom' and genuinely think that everyone will understand your mushroom desire when you produce the mushroom sentence, it would seem like Grice's theory would suggest that you *do* in fact manage to mean$_{NN}$ that you want a mushroom. You might worry that this means that insane people can mean insane things.

The second objection to Grice that I want to present here is related to this last worry. That objection is due to John Searle, who provided the following famous example:

> Suppose that I am an American soldier in WWII and that I am captured by Italian troops. And suppose also that I wish to get these troops to believe that I am a German officer in order to get them to release me. What I would like to do is to tell them in German or Italian that I am a German officer. But let us suppose I don't know enough German or Italian to do that. So I ... put on a show of telling them that I am a German officer by reciting those few bits of German that I know, trusting that they don't know enough German to see through my plan. Let us suppose I know only one line of German, which I remember from a poem I had to memorize in a high school German course. Therefore I, a captured American, address my Italian captors with the following sentence: 'Kennst du das Land, wo die Zitronen blühn'?
> (Searle 1965, 8)

In German, as Searle was fond of saying, the sentence 'Kennst du das Land, wo die Zitronen blühn'? means 'Do you know the land where the lemon trees bloom?' But when the American soldier produces the German sentence, he produces it with the intention that his audience form the belief that he is a German officer in virtue of their recognizing that intention. So it seems like Grice's theory should predict that he means$_{NN}$ that he is a German officer.

Searle himself thought that was a bizarre result – he took it to be obvious that the German sentence does not and cannot be used to mean 'I am a German officer', or anything to that effect. But he didn't take the example to be a devastating one for Grice. Searle's own view was that Grice's picture of intentions could be supplemented with a story about the role played by convention in establishing the meaning of the things we say. For Searle, someone's utterance of a sentence means a certain thing just when the:

> ... speaker intends to produce a certain effect by means of getting the hearer to recognize his intention to produce that effect, and furthermore, if he is using words literally, he intends this recognition to be achieved in virtue of the fact that the rules for using the expressions he utters associate the expressions with the production of that effect.
> (Searle 1965, 10)

Whatever the nature of the rules someone might take to apply in German (or English or Italian, for that matter), it seems clear that they will not associate the sentence 'Kennst du das Land, wo die Zitronen blühen'? with the belief that anyone is a German officer. So Searle's addendum offers a way of avoiding having to say that the American soldier can use that sentence to mean that he is a German officer. Instead of looking in more detail at the prospects for giving a version of Grice's theory of meaning that is supplemented with a clause like the one Searle proposes adding, we will turn our attention in the next section to a theory that puts conventionality in a more fundamental role.

3.2.2 LEWIS' CONVENTION-BASED THEORY

The presentation we have just given of Grice's metasemantic theory brings out the sense in which meanings for Grice are something individuals essentially will into existence in one-off events of creation. In order for something you say to mean something, there has to be someone you want to get to form a certain belief. Nothing about Grice's basic setup, however, obviously involves any reference to a broader community or to any history of past meaning-making practices.

> Does this mean we can't talk to ourselves? Or that if we do, our words wouldn't be meaningful?

Our old friend David Lewis, on the other hand, proposes a metasemantics that makes the genesis of linguistic meaning a deeply collective and historical enterprise. Recall that in Chapter One, we looked at two characterizations Lewis gave of language. The first involved the idea that languages are a certain kind of abstract object, a function that maps sentences to truth conditions. The second involved the idea that language is a certain kind of social practice, one that depends on shared assumptions about truthfulness and trust.

We said in Chapter One that these two threads are woven together by the fact that what it is for a certain language – in the sense of an abstract system of functions – to be the language spoken by a certain group of people is for those people to have a convention of trying to say only things that would be true in that language, and of trusting each other to do the same.

Now we are in a position to appreciate how those claims can be framed in metasemantic terms. Take the sentence 'it's raining', for example. If we're trying to give a metasemantics for English, part of our job will be to say what makes it the case that that sentence means that it's raining, instead of meaning that snow is white or that the sky is blue, or any other thing, or nothing at all. This question arises in part because it isn't hard to imagine a language that uses sounds (signs, etc.) just like the sound of our sentence 'it's raining' to mean one of those other things, or even for those sounds to be produced randomly by air blowing through a cave (maybe this is a little harder to imagine, but surely not impossible). Those of us who speak English will feel pretty confident that we aren't speaking one of these other languages, or doing the same thing that air whistling through a cave opening does. But what does the difference consist in?

Lewis thinks that the reason the sentence 'it's raining' means what it does for us is that our linguistic behavior is governed by a certain **convention**. One part of the convention – the truthfulness part – is that we generally only say 'it's raining' when we believe that it's raining. Another part of the convention – the trust part – is that when we hear people say 'it's raining', we take them to be doing the same thing we'd be doing if we were to say it, that is, believing that it's raining and trying only to say true things. This leads to our tending to form the belief that it's raining when we hear others utter that sentence.

These conventions are manifest in our activities – they shape the relationship between the things we say and the things we believe, and the relationship between the things we hear and the things we believe. But for Lewis, a convention is not merely a regularity in behavior. It isn't just that it *happens* to be the case that we say 'it's raining' when we believe as much and that we tend to form that belief when we hear others say it. Crucially, those tendencies are grounded both in a set of beliefs we have about how other people's speech and listening relate to their beliefs, and in the *interest* we have in having our activities and beliefs related in broadly the same way as everyone else's are.

More specifically, Lewis says that a behavioral regularity that pretty much everyone in a group conforms to becomes a convention for them when it's a regularity that has some special features. Those features are nicely illustrated by an example involving the side of the road that people drive on. In North and South America and continental Europe, cars drive on the right. This fact by itself amounts to a behavioral regularity – an alien watching from space who had no idea that cars were driven by people would be able to describe this regularity without saying anything about anyone's beliefs or desires. They could say: these two continents that are joined by a narrow isthmus are criss crossed with flat open spaces that have wheeled metallic boxes flowing in two directions, corresponding to each box's right side.

Such a description, however, would leave out something important about the way our right-hand circulation practice actually unfolds. In contrast to other behavioral regularities, like the fact that people wear more clothes when it's colder, eat and drink at fairly consistent intervals, and so on, the driving regularity is one that is *sustained* by each of us believing that the others will drive on the right, and by the fact that this belief gives us all a good reason to drive on the right ourselves (since we want to avoid collisions).

Another feature of Lewis' idea is that where conventions are concerned, we all prefer general conformity as opposed to close-to-general conformity. Think about a group of people who are such that everyone carries their wallet in their back-right pocket because they're all right-handed and it's easier to get the wallet out with their dominant hand. In such a group, there'd be a clear regularity in behavior. But it is not a regularity that anyone has a reason to prefer total conformity in than near-total conformity – I don't care at all where anyone else carries their wallet. When we drive, on the other hand, I not only prefer that *most* people stick to one side, but I prefer a situation in which 100% of the people do so to a situation in which compliance is 98%. If even a relatively small number of people drive on a different side from the majority, the roads will become dangerous, slow, and expensive for all of us.

Lewis also thinks that mutual knowledge of all of the points we've just made is important. So, in the right-hand drive parts of the world, everyone knows that everyone drives on the right, and everyone knows that everyone else knows this. Furthermore, everyone knows that this knowledge gives everyone good reasons to drive on the right and knows that everyone else knows this. Still further, everyone knows that it is better for everyone if we all stick to the right side, as opposed to mostly sticking to the right, and everyone knows that everyone knows this. This fact that knowledge is shared in this way means that all of the reasons we have for driving on the right are self-reinforcing – the interest-based reasons, for example, would be strong on their own but become even stronger when we all know that we all know that we share them.

Lewis' metasemantics is based on the idea that the situation we face with regard to language is very similar to the situation we face with regard to the side of the road we drive on. He thinks that as a matter of fact, we do, when speaking English (or any other natural language), behave in a regular fashion with regard to the way the things we believe lead us to produce certain sounds (signs, etc.), and with regard to the way the things we hear (see, etc.) lead us to produce certain beliefs. There is a robust pattern, that is, of saying 'it's raining' only when you believe that grass is green, of forming the belief that it's raining when you hear people produce that sentence, and so on.

As in the case of traffic circulation, this regularity in behavior is one that we are all familiar with, and the expectation that other people will follow it gives us all good reasons to do so ourselves. My interest in being able to share information with you – to tell you what things I like and don't like to eat, what things I want to buy or sell or whatever – combined with my expectation that our beliefs will be linked to the things we hear and say in the same way gives me a reason to conform to the regularity when I'm a speaker, and my interest in being able to gain information from you gives me a reason to conform to the regularity when I'm a listener.

If a sudden wild impulse led me to fly in the face of our behavioral regularity and begin to say 'I would like to eat a steak' whenever I wanted to eat a portobello mushroom, I would end up getting the wrong food all the time. Similarly bad results would occur if I were to break with the regularity as an interpreter. If every time someone says 'I would like to eat a steak', I form the belief that the person wants to eat a portobello mushroom, I will end up serving them the wrong food. This would be no good for either of us!

A pattern of behavior in which we can all be expected to do the same things, that is, to produce certain sentences when we hold certain beliefs and to form certain beliefs when we hear certain sentences, is a pattern that gives all of us abilities we wouldn't have otherwise – like the ability to learn about things we haven't had firsthand experience of, to coordinate our actions with others, and so on. The value of those abilities, Lewis thinks, gives each of us reasons to prefer that we all conform to the pattern in question. Of course, we know that people will sometimes lie or mislead. But even the advantage that can be gained by lying or misleading depends on the fact that for the most part, we expect everyone to be truthful and trusting – if we didn't know that people typically say 'I have no money' when they have no money, the liar who produces that sentence when it isn't true wouldn't be able to get their listeners to form the false belief that they want them to form. (If you've encountered Kant and the categorical imperative, you may see a connection here – there's a sense in which it seems like it's impossible to conceive of a situation in which everyone lied all the time; lying seems to depend on a practice of truth-telling.)

Finally, Lewis thinks that each of these points is known by all speakers of a language, and known by all to be known by all. Lewis' metasemantics, then, is summarized by the following claim:

> A language $\mathcal{L}$ is used by a population P if and only if there prevails in P a convention of truthfulness and trust in $\mathcal{L}$, sustained by an interest in communication.
> (Lewis 1975, 10)

A language, in the sense that's at stake here, is a mapping of sentences to truth conditions. So Lewis is saying that a sentence means what it does in virtue of it being mutually known that people by people in a certain population use that sentence in accordance with a convention of truthfulness and trust. In other words, a sentence means X when people know that everyone around them knows that they all utter it when they believe X and form the belief that X when they hear people utter it.

What would Lewis say to Humpty Dumpty?

FURTHER READING

Key sources for the material presented in this chapter include:

- Gareth Evans. *The Varieties of Reference*. Clarendon Press, 1982.
- Saul Kripke. *Naming and Necessity*. Harvard University Press, 1980.
- Hilary Putnam. "The meaning of 'meaning'". In: *Minnesota Studies in the Philosophy of Science* 7, (1975), pp. 131–193.

For readers who want to explore related topics in greater detail, I recommend:

- Bird, Alexander and Emma Tobin, "Natural Kinds", The Stanford Encyclopedia of Philosophy (Spring 2024 Edition), Edward N. Zalta & Uri Nodelman (eds.)
- Ruth Millikan. "Biosemantics". In: *Journal of Philosophy* 86.6 (1989), pp. 281–297.
- Fred Dretske. "Misrepresentation". In: *Belief: Form, Content, and Function*. Ed. by Radu Bogdan. Oxford University Press, 1986, pp. 17–36.
- Speaks, Jeff, "Theories of Meaning", The Stanford Encyclopedia of Philosophy (Spring 2021 Edition), Edward N. Zalta (ed.)

PRAGMATICS

A short recap covering what we have done so far will help to set up the questions we'll look at in this chapter, which will be the final piece of Part One. Recall that we began our presentation of the philosophy of language in Chapter One by looking at some very general questions about what language is and about what kinds of activities philosophers typically count as core linguistic ones. The picture we developed in that chapter, drawing in particular at several key points on David Lewis's work, was a picture on which the fundamental thing people use language to do is exchange information.

Lewis's explanation of our ability to do that involved two components. First, he said, it's important that people who share a language share knowledge of a certain kind of abstract object, a function that maps sentences (sequences of sounds or signs) to their meanings, which we modeled in terms of truth conditions. Second, and no less importantly, Lewis emphasizes that in conversation with people we think of as speaking the same language as us, we all take one another to be participating in a certain kind of shared social practice, that is, the practice of trying only to say true things and of trusting one another to do the same.

When these two conditions are met, simply by producing a particular series of sounds or producing a particular sequence of signs, I will be able to tell you things you didn't already know and learn new

DOI: 10.4324/9781003250753-4

things from you. If I produce a sentence that's true only when the world is a certain way, and you hear me, know how the world has to be to make the sentence true, and trust that I will only say things I take to be true, then you can come to know that the world is that way, or at least, that I take it to be that way, which is decent evidence for its being that way.

In Chapters Two and Three, we looked at a number of specific questions philosophers have raised about some of the components of this kind of system. In Chapter Two, we focused on semantic questions, that is, questions about what the meanings of certain expressions are and about how those meanings contribute to the truth conditions of the sentences they occur in. In Chapter Three, we took a step back and looked at metasemantic questions, that is, questions that have to do not with what expression x or y means, but why x and y have those meanings instead of some other meanings, or questions about how any linguistic objects come to have meanings in the first place.

In this chapter, we return to the general picture of communication from Chapter One, this time equipped with the concepts and the analytical tools developed in Chapters Two and Three. Our focus here will be on something philosophers and linguists call **pragmatics**. Saying exactly what pragmatics consists in is actually not easy – in particular, where to draw the border between semantics and pragmatics has been the topic of a vast literature – but the basic idea is that knowing the meanings of the words or sentences someone utters typically gets you only part of the way toward understanding what they are up to in producing them. To understand the full communicative significance of the things people say, we typically use the conventional meanings of their words as the inputs to a process of reasoning that allows us to work our way toward something richer. When doing this kind of pragmatic reasoning (which doesn't have to be explicit, and would typically not be), we take account of the context we find ourselves in (physical and social) and reflect on what the point of someone's producing a certain meaning in this context would be. For this reason, pragmatic phenomena are often said to be **post-semantic** or to involve **contextual enrichment.**

To take just a very simple illustration of this process, regardless of whether we prefer a Grice-style or a Lewis-style metasemantics, it seems clear that someone who produces the English sentence 'I am a bit chilly' says something that is true just in case they are feeling chilly. That much, you might think, is given just by the linguistic meaning of the words involved ('I' may be a special case; we'll return to it below).

To understand what someone is trying to get across when they say 'I am a bit chilly', is it enough to grasp the truth conditions associated with their sentence? Think of the kinds of motivations people typically have when they produce sentences like 'I am a bit chilly'. One of those, of course, is to get other people to form the belief that the speaker is chilly. But this motivation typically comes together with others that are more practical. I may say 'I am a bit chilly' because I want you to close the window, or because I have just seen that you closed the window and don't want you to feel that it was a selfish or inappropriate thing for you to have done, or because I want you to turn up the thermostat, or hand me a sweater, or whatever.

Of course, one way of explaining this diversity of possible messages might be to double down on the kind of theory Grice offers about meaning$_{NN}$ and say that when a person says 'I am a bit chilly' hoping to be handed a sweater, what they literally meant$_{NN}$ was 'hand me a sweater'. (Remember, for Grice, a sentence produced on an occasion means$_{NN}$ P just in case the speaker intends for the listener to come to believe P in virtue of recognizing that intention; we could amend this so that it covers more than just 'coming to believe' but also things like 'forming the desire to P' where P can involve things like handing over a sweater.)

It isn't obvious, however, that this kind of hardcore Gricean interpretation of the case is the right one. For one thing, if you say 'I am a bit chilly', and I hand you a sweater, I can also say at the same time 'Put this on, then, but it seems pretty warm to me', or even 'Are you really? You weren't chilly in the other room a second ago, and it was colder in there'. Responses like this, however, wouldn't make very much sense if what you said meant$_{NN}$ 'hand me a sweater'; after all, 'Are you really?' isn't a very natural response to 'Hand me a sweater'.

Philosophers and linguists typically say that in cases like this, you manage to do two things, in speaking. First, you say something that has the ordinary truth conditions we'd expect – in this example, that you're chilly. Additionally, however, you manage to get something else across – that you'd like the window closed, or whatever. Pragmatics is the study of how we move from the literal meanings of the things people say to a broader understanding of the way those things fit into the structures of downstream beliefs and practical consequences that they fit into. Most (all?) people working on the topic think our ability to reason pragmatically – to encode and decode these 'additional' messages – depends on the same kinds of mutually interlocking assumptions about each other's beliefs that we looked at in Chapter Three, and upon which our basic linguistic ability depends. I know I can use the sentence 'I am cold' to get you to believe that I am cold because I know that you know that I would only utter that sentence if I were cold. But I also know that I can use it to get a sweater, because if you come to have the belief that I'm cold, you'll also probably wonder why I'm telling you, see that you could fix my situation and thus win my enduring gratitude at very little cost to yourself, and so on.

4.1 CONVERSATIONAL IMPLICATURE

In a different, although amazingly, no less massively influential article from the one we looked at in Chapter Three, Grice develops an account of how it is that we are able to convey more by means of a certain sentence or expression than would be conveyed simply by its literal meaning. He provides the following example to introduce the idea:

> Suppose that A and B are talking about a mutual friend, C, who is now working in a bank. A asks B how C is getting on in his job, and B replies, *Oh quite well, I think; he likes his colleagues, and he hasn't been to prison yet.* At this point A might well inquire what B was implying, what he was suggesting, or even what he meant by saying that C had not yet been to prison. The answer might be any one of such things as that C is the sort of person likely to yield to the temptation provided by his occupation, that C's colleagues are really very unpleasant and treacherous people, and so forth.
> (Grice 1975, 43)

Like our sweater example, this vignette shows how a person can utter one sentence and manage to communicate something more than its conventional meaning. In Grice's example, it seems quite clear that speaker *A* has asserted that *C* has not yet been to prison – someone reporting *A*'s speech would definitely be providing an accurate report if they said '*A* said that *C* hasn't been to prison'.

But Grice thinks that any normal listener will also immediately see that *A* has suggested or implied something about *C*, over and above the mere fact that they haven't yet been to prison. In technical terms that Grice introduces – which are designed to allow him to sidestep debates about whether implying, suggesting, hinting, and so on all involve precisely the same phenomenon or whether there are subtle distinctions that could be drawn between them – *A* **conversationally implicates** that *C* is the sort of person who might be expected to run into legal problems while working at a bank.

Grice's analysis of the phenomenon of implicature rests on the idea that conversation is essentially a joint cooperative activity that involves the interaction of rational agents. Although my fundamental goal in talking to you might be to get you to agree to a deal that goes against your economic interests, or to get you to take a wrong turn so that my associates can steal your Cheetos, or whatever, there is a sense in which even these kinds of adversarial activities are made possible by the fact that we all behave in roughly the same ways when we speak and interpret one another and that we all know this about each other. People tend to (attempt to) say true things, that is, to believe the things others say, to answer one another's questions, and so on, and our linguistic behavior is governed by our recognition of the generality of these facts. Overall, Grice thinks, exceptions involving deception and treachery (not to mention straightforward communication that doesn't involve implicature at all) are made possible by the fact that conversations proceed according to something he calls the **cooperative principle**:

> Make your conversational contribution such as is required, at the stage at which it occurs, by the accepted purpose or direction of the talk exchange in which you are engaged.
> (Grice 1975, 45)

The cooperative principle rests on the assumption that agents involved in ordinary conversations share an intuitive sense of what the point of the conversation is – what questions are at stake, what level of detail is required to answer them, who already knows what, and so on. These mutual assumptions provide a framework that helps us to structure our own conversational contributions, and which allows us to know what to make of one another's contributions.

If we are on the street in Seoul, for example, and you, a stranger looking at a tourist map, ask me if I have been to Gwanghwamun, the kinds of answers I might provide will tend to take one set of forms, whereas if we are classmates in a Korean language class taking place in another country, those answers might turn out quite differently, due to differences in the 'accepted purpose or direction of the talk exchange' in question. In the first case, I might reply by offering you directions, while in the second I might list some of the other major attractions I'd visited.

Mixing answers of these sorts up would lead to very strange results. If you, standing in Seoul, holding the map and looking lost, ask me whether I've been to Gwanghwamun and I say 'Yes, and a picnic by the Han River is a nice idea, too', you'll probably look blankly at me. The same is true in the classroom if you ask me whether I've been and I reply 'Yes, from Seoul Station the cheapest option would be a village bus for 900 won but you could take the 1711 or the 7016, too, which come very frequently'.

While the cooperative principle is the backbone of the system Grice develops to explain the process that makes implicature possible, he supplements it with four more detailed sub-principles, which he calls the maxims of **quantity, quality, relation**, and **manner**. The maxim of quantity says to make your conversation no more or less informative than is required for the assumed purpose of the conversation. The maxim of quality says that you should try to say true things, not say things you think are false, and say only things you have evidence for. The maxim of relation says that you should make only contributions that are relevant given the point of our conversation. And the maxim of manner says that you should avoid ambiguity and obscurity, aiming to be brief and orderly in your contributions.

None of these four maxims, nor the cooperative principle they derive from, is meant to have the status of a law of nature. Grice doesn't take them to be inevitable or to provide a definition of what it is to be involved in a conversation. So, someone who fails to live up to one (or several) of the maxims doesn't thus fail to count as a conversational participant. Instead of saying what it takes to be a conversationalist at all, the point of the maxims is to specify what it takes to be a *good* one by describing the ways in which we actually tend to organize our speech. Since we generally follow them, know that everyone else does too, and know that everyone knows as much, violations of the maxims will be jarring. If you go to a place where everyone begins dancing by leading with their left foot, and where everyone knows that everyone knows this, then for you to lead with your right foot will mean that in addition to your stepping on a lot of toes, you'll give people the impression either that you're clueless or that you're doing it on purpose.

In the case of conversation, this latter possibility is the interesting one. Grice's four maxims of conversation really start to do theoretical work when we think about the consequences of breaking them, *despite* everyone's recognition of the central role they play in organizing our linguistic exchanges. There are three ways in which such violations can occur.

The first of these involves being sneaky, violating one of the maxims without doing anything that would tip others off to the fact that the maxim has been violated. For example, if I start saying things that I in fact think are false but don't give any indication that I think that, and do so in a context in which you don't have any obvious reason to think that I'm doing it, then I'll end up misleading you. Since you assume that I'm following the maxim of quality, you will assume that I believe and have evidence for the things I say, and will thus end up with believing some things that are untrue or which you don't have adequate support for.

The second way in which someone might break with the maxims is to explicitly point out that they will violate one, as when I ask you a question concerning an experience I know you had, and you say 'I'm sorry but I can't answer that – on this topic, my lips are sealed', or something similar. In this case, although I know that you have the information I want, you decline to provide it, and thus fail to live up to the maxim of quantity. When this kind of violation occurs, the conversation either ends or the topic changes, and while listeners will certainly be in a position to make assumptions about the reasons for the speaker's silence, Grice doesn't think there is a systematic way of reading a particular sort of message into cases with this structure.

Finally, and most interestingly, we can violate the maxims *ostentatiously but not necessarily explicitly*, violating one (or several) in a way that we know others will notice, but which provides them no reason to think that we mean to be done with the conversation or that we mean to be uncooperative or misleading. In this kind of case, Grice says, a speaker can consciously exploit the cooperative principle in order to send a message that goes beyond the literal meaning of the words they utter. This is the mechanism at work in the case of conversational implicature, the core phenomenon Grice's article aims to explain.

Specifically, Grice defines the phenomenon of conversational implicature as follows:

> [Someone] who, by (in, when) saying (or making as if to say) that *P* has implicated that *Q*, may be said to have conversationally implicated that *Q* PROVIDED THAT (1) they are presumed to be observing the conversational maxims, or at least the cooperative principle, (2) the supposition that they are aware that, or thinks that, *Q* is required in order to make their saying or making as if to say *P* (or doing so in THOSE terms) consistent with this presumption; and (3) the speaker thinks (and would expect the hearer to think the speaker to think that the speaker thinks) that it is within the competence of the hearer to work out, or grasp intuitively, that the supposition mentioned in (2) is required.
> (Grice 1975, 49-50)

While Grice's formulation may not be completely in keeping with his own maxim of manner, the basic idea is straightforward enough. Let's see how it would apply to the example we began with, that is, the example involving someone who responds to a question about how a mutual friend is getting on at their new banking job by saying 'well, they haven't been to prison yet!'

On the face of things, this answer seems like a total non-sequitur. If I ask how a certain person is doing after being hired to work in a bank, and you reply with something about prison, that seems like a clear violation of the maxim of relation, which says that speakers should be relevant. Unless it's mutually known that the person in question has often ended up in prison while working at previous jobs, though, it doesn't seem like your answer even minimally addresses my question.

So what should I do as an interpreter? One option would be to treat you as uncooperative – to conclude that you're just saying any random thing that pops into your mind, not even trying to fit your contributions into the logical back-and-forth of the conversation I want to have, a conversation whose aims and structure would be apparent to any normal interlocutor. But another option would be for me to reflect on whether there might be some other message that you're trying to get me to see. If you haven't given me other reasons to think that you're violating the cooperative principle – you're not obviously drunk or mumbling incoherently, you're looking at me as though I should understand your contribution, etc. – Grice thinks it'll typically make sense for me to take this stance.

Then the key question for me as an interpreter becomes: what other message could you have been aiming to send? Although the literal content associated with the sentence you produced was irrelevant, I can ask whether there is some *other* proposition in the vicinity that would make your contribution relevant, and which you could have reasonably expected me to be able to deduce. If there is a proposition that would meet these two criteria, Grice thinks you conversationally implicate it by answering my question with your apparently unrelated answer. In the case of the bank example, he thinks that the proposition that the person we are talking about is the kind of person who might be tempted toward dishonesty meets this standard:

> In a suitable setting A might reason as follows: '(1) B has apparently violated the maxim 'Be relevant' and so may be regarded as having flouted one of the maxims conjoining perspicuity, yet I have no reason to suppose that he is opting out from the operation of the CP; (2) given the circumstances, I can regard his irrelevance as only apparent if, and only if, I suppose him to think that C is potentially dishonest; (3) B knows that I am capable of working out step (2). So B implicates that C is potentially dishonest.
> (Grice 1975, 50)

Before stepping back to critically evaluate Grice's proposal, let's take a moment to make sure we're all on the same page by looking at a few more examples of conversational implicature. One that comes up very frequently in discussions of the topic involves a letter of recommendation. Suppose that someone who recently finished their PhD in philosophy is applying for academic jobs. As a standard part of the process, letters of recommendation are required. The student asks their dissertation advisor to submit such a letter, which they do, and the content reads entirely as follows:

> Dear Search Committee Member:
> My student X's handwriting is excellent, they never make mistakes in spelling, and their attendance at tutorial meetings has been regular.
> Very best,
> Advisor

It seems very clear that a letter of this sort will not help the job candidate's case, or at least, will not help if we assume that the reader of the letter trusts the author to be a good judge of philosophical aptitude and an honest and cooperative source of testimony on this occasion.

Grice's theory of conversational implicatures offers an explanation of this fact. Grice takes the letter to be evidence that the author is behaving according to the cooperative principle – if they were not, why would they bother to write at all? Furthermore, he takes it to be part of the common ground that the letter writer is in a good position to provide detailed feedback about their student's philosophical talent – the author has worked closely with the applicant for years! – and that a candid assessment is what is wanted by the reader, since that's the whole point of the practice of submitting letters of recommendation.

On the face of things, however, it seems like the author is failing to provide the kind of information that's required by the accepted purpose of the conversation – the information seems to be of the wrong kind, in that it completely overlooks the question of philosophical aptitude, and of an insufficient volume, since so little is provided. In Grice's terms, then, we have candidate violations of the maxims of relation (be relevant!) and of quantity (be as informative as is required!) on our hands.

Since these violations are so blatant, and since they come in a context that suggests that the letter writer isn't meaning to be uncooperative, Grice takes it that the person reading the letter will realize that there must be another message that the author wants to communicate but doesn't feel comfortable writing out explicitly.

'This supposition', Grice says, 'is tenable only on the assumption that... X is no good at philosophy' Grice (1975), pg 52. So, by his definition, the letter writer conversationally implicates that X is no good at philosophy.

Philosophers and linguists widely agree that something like Grice's notion of conversational implicature is a very important part of our everyday practice of using language. We often intend to communicate more than we strictly say, that is, counting on the fact that our listeners will be able to calculate the 'hidden' contents we have in mind. In general terms, it seems hard to dispute that Grice has outlined the structure of the reasoning that must underlie this ability: X said something that seems irrelevant, or over- or under-detailed, or whatever. If I take X's words at face value, they violate ordinary expectations about how a conversation should be structured. But if I treat them as meaning this other thing instead, they would suddenly snap into relevance, provide the right level of detail, and so on. So, I should treat them as meaning that other thing!

If we look at the details, however, it becomes less obvious whether Grice's account gets things quite right. As Grice sets up his theory, recall, the key claim isn't just that P conversationally implicates Q if the conventional meaning of P would violate the conversational maxims, but treating it as though it meant Q would repair the violation. His claim is that P conversationally implicates Q if it's *necessary* for avoiding the violation that we treat P as though it meant Q. To conversationally implicate Q by means of a sentence P, then, the situation has to be set up in such a way that there is no other proposition Z such that treating P as though it meant Z would fix the problem.

This 'necessity requirement' places a very high bar on implicatures, and it isn't clear that Grice's own examples meet it. Recall the example we began with, of the conversation A and B have about C, who has recently begun working in a bank. When addressing the question of what B might have been implying or suggesting by saying that C hadn't been to prison yet, Grice writes:

> The answer might be any one of such things as that C is the sort of person likely to yield to the temptation provided by his occupation, that C's colleagues are really very unpleasant and treacherous people, and so forth. (Grice 1975, 43)

When explaining why it is that B's sentence about C's not yet having been sent to prison implicates that C is the sort of person who is potentially dishonest, Grice says that B's answer can be made relevant 'if and only if I suppose him to think that C is potentially dishonest'.

But is this right? Grice himself seems to provide a counterexample – maybe C is very honest but has treacherous colleagues who themselves are not honest and who would be well suited by having a rookie scapegoat around to blame when money goes missing. To know which of these two propositions – that C is dishonest, or that C is honest but the others are not – a listener is more likely to arrive at, we'd have to hear more about the background circumstances against which the conversation takes place. But the mere fact that we can imagine two possible ways of framing B's utterance, each of which would make it relevant, and neither of which seems to entail the other, suggests that neither of them is necessary, which means that by Grice's definition, neither should be conversationally implicated by what B says.

The difference between 'treating P as though it meant Q is necessary to make sense of the speaker' and 'treating P as though it meant Q would make sense of the speaker' comes up in the other examples we've looked at, too. When reading the letter of recommendation, treating the author as someone who wants to tell me that their student is no good at philosophy is clearly one way of making sense of them. But wouldn't it also make sense of them to treat them as though they wanted me to know that their student has some grave character flaw? While it seems plausible that most of us will arrive at the 'this student is no good' interpretation more easily than we will arrive at other interpretations, it doesn't seem like that is the only one that would make sense of the letter writer or that all of the ways of making sense of them involve the idea that the student is no good (maybe the author thinks the job is below the standards of the student and expects the reader to be able to see as much).

Again, to be clear, these points do little to undermine the importance of the phenomenon Grice has pointed out. But they are something to consider when you think about implicature. It seems clear that the standard 'anything that would make sense of your interlocutor is implicated by them' is too weak, since there are many whacky interpretations that would in theory make sense of someone's speech behavior in any given context. But the standard 'required to make sense of' seems overly demanding. As in so many places in philosophy, then, it seems like the Goldilocks principle must apply here, and that the trick for us in developing a theory of implicature will be to find the happy middle ground.

Try to come up with a few examples of implicatures on your own or find some videos of dialogue that involve communication via implicature. Are the implicated propositions *necessary* to make sense of the speaker? Would some other proposition work for that purpose? Would it work as well as the proposition you found? Spell out the steps of a Gricean explanation in detail, specifying which maxim is violated and how your proposed implicated content would repair the violation.

4.2 CONTEXTUAL ENRICHMENT

Another area in which there seems to be a kind of gap between the conventional or 'dictionary' meanings of the words we use and the things that people will take us to have said concerns what philosophers and linguists call **context-sensitive** language. Articles on context sensitivity often start with a short list of paradigmatically context-sensitive expressions to help the reader see what kind of phenomenon is at stake. Those lists often involve expressions like 'you, I, here, now' in one group, and expressions like 'he, she, they, this, that, those' in another.

What makes all of these expressions context-sensitive is the fact that they seem to pick out different objects in different contexts. So, when *I* say 'I am cold', most people will have the intuition that I say something about myself, but when *you* say 'I am cold', most people will have the intuition that you say something about you. In short: same word, different context, different apparent referent. The situation is similar with 'this', 'that', and so on. When I say 'This is tasty', holding a cookie, ordinary listeners will take me to be talking about the cookie. If I use the same sentence holding a piece of surströmming, a sort of fermented herring popular in Sweden, listeners will take me to be talking about the herring. Again: same word, different context, different referent.

Philosophers have traditionally been interested in a difference between these two groups of context-sensitive expressions. On the one hand, words like 'you, I, here, now', which philosophers call **indexicals** seem to have their referents determined in a way that is 'automatic' in a certain sense. Regardless of what I'm thinking about, or intending to talk about, or doing with my body, it seems quite clear that when I produce the word 'I', it refers to me; when I produce the word 'now', it refers to the time at which I produce it; when I produce the word 'here' it refers to the place I'm located, and so on.

Can you think of any exceptions to these generalizations? Does 'I' always refer to the speaker? Does 'here' always refer to the place of utterance?

For example, when Rip van Winkle wakes up after two hundred years sleeping, he has no idea where in time he is. But if he says 'Wow, now I'm really hungry' or 'What time is it now?', we take him to be talking about the time of his utterance. Suppose he was moved to a safe location during his long sleep. If he says, after waking up, 'It's really nice here, where am I?', we take him to be talking about the place he's located, even if there's a sense in which he has no idea where that place is.

Words like 'this' and 'that', and compounds involving them like 'this sack of flour' and 'that bristlecone pine', on the other hand, which philosophers call **demonstratives**, appear not to involve this same kind of automaticity. Suppose we are at the park and there is a group of dogs running happily and freely in a certain area. I say, without giving any indication of which dog I mean 'That's a lovely pup, isn't it?' In a case like this, interpreters won't know what to do — unlike in the case of 'I' or 'now', here it seems that which dog I'm talking about is at least partially determined by which dog I'm thinking about. You might reply 'Which dog do you mean?', assuming that I do in fact mean to talk about a particular dog, and that the dog I meant to talk about is the one I did in fact refer to. If I was thinking about or had my attention focused on Peggy, it seems natural to say that I was talking about Peggy, if I was thinking about Buxton, it seems natural to say that I was talking about Buxton, and so on.

The issues raised by the phenomenon of context sensitivity generally, as well as by this distinction between (automatic) indexicals and (non-automatic) demonstrative expressions are large and complicated, and unfortunately we don't have time to look at them in more detail here. Although it's important to be aware of potential differences, for our purposes the key thing to notice is something that applies to both groups: there is a sense in which understanding someone who uses a context-sensitive expression requires no more than that you share a language with them, and a sense in which understanding what someone says by means of a context sensitive expression also requires that you know some things about the context you're in.

To bring these two senses out more clearly, consider an example. Suppose you travel to a foreign country where you speak the language, but where your traveling companion does not. You come across a piece of ancient graffiti in that language, which says the equivalent of 'Today it rained and my shoes got wet. Woe is me!'. Your friend sees the graffiti and asks if you understand what it means. Supposing you have no idea who the author was, or when the graffiti was written, it seems like there is a sense in which you can say 'yes', and a sense in which you have to say 'no'.

What do these two senses consist in, exactly? So far, remember, we have been working under the assumption that knowing the meaning of a sentence is knowing its truth conditions. The graffiti example, however, suggests that at least where sentences involving context-sensitive expressions are concerned, the picture might need to be made a bit more complicated.

In this case, it seems pretty clear that you do not know the truth conditions associated with the sentence. If I put a set of cards in front of you with all of the possible worlds on them, you wouldn't be able to sort them into a pile of cards that contain the worlds in which the thing the author said was true, and the set in which it's false. (You could, of course, put all the worlds in which it never rains in the false pile, and all the worlds in which it's always raining and everyone's shoes are always wet in the true pile, but that would leave you with a lot of cards.)

At the same time, though, it also seems clear that just in virtue of knowing the language, you know something important about the sentence's truth conditions that your friend doesn't know. You might not know the truth conditions themselves, but you know what we might think of as a *recipe* for figuring those truth conditions out, given some information about the context of utterance. If the sentence was produced by Jisoo on 11 January 1845, for example, and you know the language involved, you'll be able to confidently say that the sentence is true just in case Jisoo's shoes were soaked by rain on that day, and false otherwise. If the sentence was produced by Hueiya on 6 June 1918, you'll know it's true just in case Hueiya's shoes were soaked by rain on that day, and so on. (It's important to emphasize here that truth conditions aren't the same as the truth value of the sentence; if you know who said it and when, you know the truth conditions. But to actually know whether the sentence is true or false, you need to know whether it was raining and whether someone's shoes got wet.)

David Kaplan, a UCLA philosopher and logician, became very famous for developing a model of meaning that allows us to distinguish these two senses. On the one hand, Kaplan said, we have the 'recipe' kind of meaning, which he calls **character**. Formally, Kaplan models character as a function that takes a sentence and a context and gives you a fuller kind of meaning, which he called **content**. While the details aren't important for us here, Kaplan held that contents fix the truth conditions associated with a sentence as it's used on a particular occasion.

This complicates the picture of meaning that we started with, on which people who know a language know a rule that associates sentence types with truth conditions. But the complication is one that seems well justified by the facts, and also conservative in the sense that it preserves the basic structure of the view we began with. Nowadays, many philosophers think that the linguistic meaning or 'timeless' meaning associated with a sentence type is given by its Kaplanian character. To understand what people are trying to communicate when they speak, however, we need to grasp not just the character, but the content associated with the token sentence produced.

Getting a content out of a character involves a pragmatic process, a process of enrichment. In virtue of knowing English, you know that 'I' refers to the person speaking or signing, 'here' refers to the place at which the speech or signs are produced, 'that' to the object the speaker is pointing at, thinking about, or whatever. When you encounter someone using context-sensitive expressions, in order to come up with truth conditions, you need to add some extra-linguistic bulk to the linguistic skeleton they provide you with. In ordinary circumstances, a speaker will assume that you know they are the one talking, assume that you know where the speech is taking place, and so on. They know, that is, that your knowledge of the extra-linguistic context will allow you to move from the linguistic meanings of the expressions they produce to their truth conditions.

FURTHER READING

Key sources for the material presented in this chapter include:

- Herbert Paul Grice. "Logic and conversation". In: *Syntax and Semantics 3: Speech Acts*. Ed. by Peter Cole and Jerry Morgan. Cambridge, MA: Academic Press, 1975, pp. 41–58.

For readers who want to explore related topics in greater detail, I recommend:

- Braun, David, "Indexicals", The Stanford Encyclopedia of Philosophy (Summer 2017 Edition), Edward N. Zalta (ed.)
- Davis, Wayne, "Implicature", The Stanford Encyclopedia of Philosophy (Spring 2024 Edition), Edward N. Zalta & Uri Nodelman (eds.)
- Korta, Kepa and John Perry, "Pragmatics", The Stanford Encyclopedia of Philosophy (Spring 2020 Edition), Edward N. Zalta (ed.)
- Robert Stalnaker. "Assertion". In: *Syntax and Semantics* 9 (1978), pp. 315–332.

Part II

SPEECH AS ACTION

SPEECH ACT THEORY

5.1 INTRODUCTION

Until relatively recently, if you had taken a course in the philosophy of language at a major US or UK university, the material presented would have looked very much like the material we have covered here so far in Part One – Frege's Hesperus/Phosphorus puzzle, Kripke's causal-historical treatment of proper names, Grice's intention-based theory of meaning and its extension to cover conversational implicatures, together with the other topics we took up have been the bread and butter for teachers in the philosophy of language for a long time. In the last 20 years or so, however, more and more philosophers have been exploring questions about language and language use from a social and political perspective. The literature that has resulted from this newer focus is extremely diverse both in terms of the questions themselves that are raised and in terms of the theoretical approaches involved in formulating answers to them, and no single book, let alone part of a book, could do justice to all or even most of it.

Instead of trying to give a comprehensive survey of work in this area, our aim here will be similar to the one we set ourselves in Part One, that is, to consider a series of contributions that will equip us with the kinds of theoretical tools that would be required to read more widely in an independent way. Many of those tools will in fact

DOI: 10.4324/9781003250753-5

carry over from Part One. For example, where political and ethical questions about the importance of freedom of speech are concerned, the picture we developed there of communication as a rational activity made possible by mutual knowledge of a semantic theory and by interpersonal cooperation will continue to be a useful one. Appreciating the structure of that picture puts us in a good position to appreciate ways in which threats to free speech might be manifest – not only overt restrictions (e.g., legal or physical threats) could undermine communicative exchange, but indeed, anything that made it less likely that people see one another as good faith participants in a Lewis-style practice of truth and trust. It's similarly straightforward to frame issues of justice in terms of the classic model of communication – suppose a certain visible minority group's social identity makes it less likely that members' utterances allow them to affect others' beliefs by speaking. That seems like it'd be a serious problem!

While many of the topics we'll look at in Part Two will continue to draw on the background we established in Part One, however, there is an idea that runs through many of those topics that we *haven't* looked at yet: the idea that in speaking, we not only exchange information with one another but perform actions that affect the relationships we stand in, among other things. That idea will be the focus of our discussion in this chapter, and in the chapters to follow we will look at a range of different contexts in which it has played an important role.

5.2 AUSTIN AND PERFORMATIVE UTTERANCES

Although versions of the thought that speaking involves performing a kind of action can be discerned at least as far back as Frege – who took it to be one thing for a sentence to encode a certain meaning, and another for the sentence to be *used* by someone to endorse that meaning – it is nowadays often associated with the work of the Oxford philosopher J.L. Austin. Austin's most famous contribution was the development of something we typically now call **speech act theory**, which, as the name suggests, is built around the idea that we use language not only to exchange information but to do things to, for, and in front of one another.

Presentations of Austin's work often begin with the observation that there is a category of sentences that look on the surface just like the kinds of sentences we use to provide reports about matters of fact, but which seem not to be used for that purpose. In his own words, the theory he aims to develop is focused on 'a kind of utterance which looks like a statement, which is not nonsensical, and yet is not true or false' (1962, 235).

Some examples will help to bring this idea out. Consider a person who is participating in a wedding. When the right moment in the ceremony comes, the officiant asks 'Do you take this person to be your lawfully-wedded spouse?' and the participant responds 'I do' – that is, 'I do take the person in front of me to be my lawfully-wedded spouse'. Or imagine a person smashing a bottle of champagne on the bow of a newly build ship and saying 'I name this ship the *Queen Elizabeth*'!

About these examples, Austin writes:

> In all these cases it would be absurd to regard the thing that I say as a report of the performance of the action which is undoubtedly done – the action of betting, or christening, or apologizing. We should say rather that, in saying what I do, I actually perform that action. When I say 'I name this ship the *Queen Elizabeth*' I do not describe the christening ceremony, I actually perform the christening; and when I say 'I do'... I am not reporting on a marriage, I am indulging in it.
> (Austin 1962, 235)

In terms that he is responsible for introducing into the philosophical lexicon, Austin calls utterances like these **performative utterances**. The distinguishing feature of a performative utterance is that instead of providing a report about how things are, it *makes* things a certain way. When a police officer says 'you are under arrest', that is, they aren't providing you with a report about how things are in the world – their utterance (together with a background set of social facts that make it possible for them to use that utterance in the right way) is itself what makes it the case that you are under arrest. If they hadn't said the words, you wouldn't be under arrest! The same goes for judges who say 'you are guilty', umpires who say 'that's a strike!' and so on.

While he doesn't endorse any hard-and-fast rules about this, Austin points out that it is generally possible to identify the kinds of sentences he takes to involve performativity by means of some grammatical features. The most prominent of these has come to be called the **hereby test** – can you insert the word 'hereby' before the main verb of a sentence? If so, that's at least a clue that you have a performative utterance on your hands. Think about the examples we've seen so far: I (hereby) take this person to be my partner; I (hereby) name this ship the *Queen Elizabeth*. Those sound quite natural, don't they? Indeed, a very wide variety of verbs admit 'hereby', and it seems plausible that most or all of them involve actions in Austin's sense; to mention just a few more, consider 'I hereby promise', 'I hereby apologize', and 'I hereby bet that...'.

> Can you think of some examples of your own? That is, can you find a verb that can follow 'hereby' naturally and seems to involve the performance of a kind of action? Can you think of words that take 'hereby' but don't seem to involve a performance?

Nevertheless – and we will look at a variety of cases in more detail in the chapters to come – philosophers (including Austin himself) have given reasons for thinking that there are performative utterances that don't pass this test. Much recent work on slurs and pejorative expressions, for example, which can't be set off by 'hereby', holds that people who use them perform a kind of action that can't be fully explained in terms of message sending (others disagree; we'll take up this question in Chapter Seven). Nevertheless, the test can be useful to keep in mind when thinking about whether some expression is performative or not.

5.2.1 EXPLAINING PERFORMATIVITY AWAY?

To bring out how distinctive his view is, Austin contrasts it with an alternative that would preserve the shape of the information-exchange picture of language we developed in Part One. Suppose someone were to disagree with the claim that what Austin calls 'performatives' really involve a special kind of action. Suppose, that is, that they insist that when you utter the words 'I do (take this person to be my lawful wedded partner)' or 'I apologize', you are merely providing a report about the state of the world. What part of the world might you be reporting about? What kind of facts, that is, would make your utterance true or false?

One natural thing to try and say might be that utterances like these turn out true or false on the basis of the way things are with you – presumably you have to be willing to marry someone in order to count as married, and maybe you have to (at least in some sense?) feel sorry in order to count as apologetic. Would it be enough, then, to analyze Austin's alleged performatives by claiming that when someone says 'I do', they are providing a report about their willingness, or that when they say 'Sorry!' they are providing a report about the presence of an internal state of regret? Could it be that when the police officer says 'you're under arrest', they've already changed the legal facts somehow and are now simply informing you about the change?

We'll come back to these points later in the chapter in a bit more detail, but against this sort of idea, note that it doesn't seem right to say that being willing to marry someone makes it the case that you are married; much of tragedy consists precisely in the fact that one person was willing to marry another, but that was not enough to make them count as married, or that two people were willing to marry one another, but could not. The same goes for apologizing – while we do typically take it to be true that people who apologize in fact regret or feel bad about the thing they're apologizing for, simply regretting or feeling bad about something doesn't make it true that you've apologized – it's even possible for someone to truthfully say 'I regret and feel bad about that, but I refuse to apologize'.

If being in mental states like this isn't enough to count as providing the content for reports like the ones we've looked at, could there be a certain kind of inner mental action that would do the trick? Could we say that it isn't just that you are willing to be married, in the sense of thinking that a marriage would be a good thing, or the thing to do, but that you in fact somehow actually perform an action of the will that results in your counting as married? Maybe this could help with the police officer example, too – while arresting someone seems pretty clearly not to depend on any particular belief held by an officer, maybe there is some way of directing their will such that when police do it, they cause someone to be arrested, which they then tell arrested people about after?

Austin thinks this is obviously a wrong way of going, for reasons similar to the ones we've just seen. Even if you and your partner both close your eyes and think to yourselves 'let us now be married!', this will not count as constituting a marriage from the perspective of the tax or immigration authorities, and your family will likely not count it for much, either. Similarly, you can will that a ship come to have a certain name, or that an apology be made, or whatever, but unless you actually pronounce the magic words, you won't end up married, the ship won't end up named, and so on. If your parents tell you that you have to apologize to your younger sibling after doing something you shouldn't have, you can't truly say 'I already did' on the basis of an internal action you performed. And my understanding of the law is that you are not under arrest if no one says 'you're under arrest' – so it can't be the case that at the time the utterance is produced, you were under arrest.

5.3 FELICITY CONDITIONS – HOW PERFORMANCES CAN FAIL

Seeing that the class of utterances Austin focuses on cannot be treated as reports, either about people's dispositions in general or about internal actions they undertake, brings us back to the heart of his view: the idea that instead of there being two things, one an action and the second a report about it, where performative utterances are concerned, there is just one thing: your saying 'I do' *constitutes* your agreeing to be married, your saying 'I name this ship the *Queen Elizabeth*' constitutes the naming, and so on. What it is to apologize is to say the words 'I apologize', and what it is to arrest someone is to say the words 'You are under arrest'.

It is important to be clear, however, that the idea that pronouncing a certain set of words amounts to the performance of a certain action doesn't mean that the only thing required to perform the action is to utter the words. Consider a comparison between speech act theory and legal practice. On Austin's telling, which not being a lawyer myself I will have to take for granted, contracts typically involve two distinct components: one is the preamble and the other an 'operative' clause or set of clauses. The preamble describes a set of background circumstances that we might think of as describing the conditions in which the operative clause can be 'activated'. I might, for example, write 'His being my only brother and having been deprived of the better part of our inheritance for so many years due to our parents' unequal disposition, I hereby give and bequeath my binoculars to NN'.

If it is true that I have just one brother, NN, and that he was deprived of the better part of our inheritance for the reasons described in the contract, then when I put my signature on it, I bring the operative clause to life and thus make it the case that ownership of the binoculars transfers to him. If, on the other hand, it turns out that there was an unknown third brother or that the brother I know in fact secretly inherited more than I did, then the operative clause, whether I sign it or not, will have no power to change the legal landscape in the way it otherwise would have.

To put the same point in slightly different terms, we might think of the preamble as describing the conditions under which a certain magic spell can be cast – it has to be the full moon, you have to be a magician, you have to have the feathers of an Arctic tern in your pocket, and so on. Then the words of the spell themselves – the words the magician utters when casting it – provide something analogous to the operative clause. Simply by uttering them, the magician summons whatever they aim to summon or makes disappear whatever they aim to make disappear. But if the moon isn't full, or you aren't a magician, or you don't have the feathers of an Arctic tern in their pocket, uttering the words of the spell won't amount to casting it.

This distinction between the preamble and the operative clause of a contract or between the circumstances under which a certain spell can be cast by producing some words and the nature of the words themselves allows us to understand some of the ways in which things can go wrong where speech acts are concerned. Austin calls cases in which someone utters a form of words that would normally constitute the performance of a certain kind of action but in which that action fails to be realized **infelicities**, and much of the philosophical richness of his account and of later work that draws on it consists in an exploration of the way such infelicities occur and of the consequences of their occurring.

On Austin's characterization, infelicities come in two basic flavors. Some are serious enough that they mean that the speech act someone was attempting to perform simply doesn't get performed. In other cases, he says, the speech act counts as having been performed but ends up being defective somehow.

While there are in principle many ways in which a speech act might be fatally flawed – that is, in which someone's uttering 'the magic words' might utterly fail to amount to the kind of performance that was intended – three will be particularly important for us over the course of the chapters to come. I will call these the **background requirement**, the **procedural requirement**, and the **uptake requirement**. The divisions between the three as I'll characterize them here will be a bit arbitrary, and they bleed into one another a bit, but naming them this way will nevertheless help to draw attention to some important features of the terrain.

5.3.1   THE BACKGROUND REQUIREMENT

The **background requirement** is meant to capture the idea that in order for an utterance to count as the performance of a speech act, the circumstances in which it is uttered have to be a certain way. We have already seen, in the cases of the contract and the magic spell, some examples of how the background requirement might work; contracts typically only enter into force when certain conditions are met, and (according to standard rules in fiction) spells often require more than just that certain words be uttered.

As with contracts and magic spells, so with the myriad kinds of speech acts we perform in daily life. While most of those acts don't involve anything so explicitly formulated as the terms of a contract's preamble, or so uncommon as a full moon and a pocket of Arctic tern feathers, they nevertheless depend quite clearly on a network of assumptions about which kinds of people can do which kinds of things (and in the case of speech acts that affect others, to which kinds of people). In Austin's formulation, they depend on the existence of a set of conventions that everyone, or most people, or the relevant people accept. Consider the following examples:

> Suppose that, picking sides at a children's party, I say 'I pick George'. But George turns red in the face and says 'Not playing'. In that case I plainly, for some reason or another, have not picked George – whether because there is no convention that you can pick people who aren't playing, or because George in the circumstances isn't an inappropriate object for the procedure of picking. Or consider the case in which I say 'I appoint you Consul', and it turns out that you have been appointed already – or perhaps it may even transpire that you are a horse; here again we have the infelicity of inappropriate circumstances, inappropriate objects, or what not.
> (Austin 1962, 238)

Whether implicitly or explicitly, we all accept that you can only pick someone to play on your team in an impromptu game if you are the captain, and if the person in question has agreed to play, and so on. If you say 'I pick Zlatan', but Zlatan isn't nearby or hasn't agreed to play, the fact that you've used the form of words we'd normally take to constitute someone's being placed on your team doesn't cut any ice. The same goes if you aren't the captain – if Zlatan is here and is playing, but you are just a random bystander or even a team member who isn't empowered to make picks, no amount of saying 'I pick Zlatan' will make him part of the team. Although there is nothing more for the appropriately-positioned person to do in order to pick someone than to say 'I pick you', that is, the words only work when a certain set of background conditions are met. What is it to count as empowered to make picks? This will be a complicated question in the philosophy of mind and social philosophy, but for our purposes, it will be enough to say that everyone involved takes you to have that authority – there is an agreement that the picking convention is one you can partake of.

The same basic points hold in the case of the Consul, and indeed, in our speech act practices generally. Anyone can say 'I appoint you Consul', but only in the mouth of someone who is appropriately socially positioned do those words realize an appointment. And then, only when the person being appointed isn't already Consul and isn't a horse. To vote by using the words 'I vote with the majority!' you have to be a member of the organization holding the vote, and to place someone under arrest by saying 'You are under arrest', you have to be a police officer. To make a legally binding promise you have to be of the appropriate age, although you may be able to make socially binding promises before that. We don't normally, however, allow people to make promises on other peoples' behalf, however old they are, and it's debatable whether you can make a promise to a non-human animal.

5.3.2   THE PROCEDURAL REQUIREMENT

The second requirement that has to be met in order for a certain speech act to be realized according to Austin's theory is the **procedural requirement**. This requirement is supposed to capture the idea that certain types of action are characteristically associated with certain forms of expression. We might formulate it by saying that in order to realize one of these speech acts, we have to follow the procedure in question accurately and completely.

Consider the expressions 'No, thanks!' and 'Yes, please!', for example. These expressions are associated with certain speech acts by convention – the first is used to refuse an offer and the second to accept. Imagine a circumstance in which the host at a party is offering you more potato salad. You have two clearly defined options in speech act terms: accept or refuse. You want to accept, and you intend to utter the words 'Yes, please!' but due to a weird slip of the tongue or a distant neuroscientist's remote intervention, 'No, thanks!' comes out.

In a case like this, Austin will say – and I imagine most readers will agree – that you have not accepted the host's offer. The speech act you intended to perform fails because your speech didn't conform to the accepted procedure, and in virtue of the procedural facts (to accept you have to say 'Yes' and to refuse 'No'), you count as having refused.

Of course, the actual procedure for accepting and refusing in English (and presumably in most languages) is one that countenances a wide variety of different forms – the convention in question involves a degree of flexibility. So, in addition to 'No, thanks!' and 'Yes, please!', you can realize refusals and acceptances by saying things like 'It was delicious, but I'm stuffed' or 'I'm stuffed, but there's always room for more potato salad', or whatever. Where the speech acts of accepting and refusing are concerned, the procedural requirement is fairly loose (even if not so loose that they let 'No thanks' could count as an acceptance).

In other cases, things are more strict. In order to have a degree conferred upon you by the University of Oxford, for example, you must utter the words *do fidem* at the right part of the ceremony. If, when the officiant asks whether you swear to follow all the rules of the University you say 'Why not?' or 'Sure thing, mate', you will not be counted as having sworn, since the procedure requires a specific form of words.

In an interesting real-world case that unfolded along similar lines, a number of politicians associated with the pro-democracy movement in Hong Kong attracted the attention of international media in October 2016 by speaking in a way that pushed the boundaries of Austin's procedural condition on speech acts. At that time, in order to officially become a member of the Hong Kong Legislative Council, people who won district elections were required to read the following oath:

> I swear that, being a member of the Legislative Council of the Hong Kong Special Administrative Region of the People's Republic of China, I will uphold the Basic Law of the Hong Kong Special Administrative Region of the People's Republic of China, bear allegiance to the Hong Kong Special Administrative Region of the People's Republic of China and serve the Hong Kong Special Administrative Region conscientiously, dutifully, in full accordance with the law, honestly and with integrity.

When the time came to read the oath in the Council chamber, a group of election winners chose to do so in striking ways. Leung Kwok-hung, for example, read the text while carrying a yellow umbrella with protest slogans written on it, and Lau Siu-lai read it over the course of 10 minutes, syllable for syllable, with long pauses in between. Leung Chung-hang and Yau Wai-ching pronounced the word 'China' in a way that has derogatory associations, and other election winners made political statements before or after the oath.

In this case, the people speaking were all appropriately positioned to realize the speech act of oath-taking – they won elections in the districts they were to represent. Each of them read each of the words from the oath out loud, and in the right sequence. But the highest judicial committee of the People's Republic of China intervened, issuing an interpretation of the article of the Hong Kong Basic Law that describes the procedure for oaths of office in a way that disqualified their readings. According to the committee, to take the oath required not simply that an election-winner read each word but that they read them 'solemnly and sincerely'. As a result of this intervention, Nathan Law, Lau Siu-lai, Edward Yiu and Leung Kwok-hung were prevented from taking seats in the Legislative Council, and others were required to retake the oath.

5.3.3   THE UPTAKE REQUIREMENT

The third and final requirement an utterance has to meet in order to count as the performance of a speech act on Austin's account is the **uptake requirement**. Exactly what kind of uptake is required for what kinds of speech acts is a matter of substantial debate in the philosophical literature, but we can introduce the idea by looking at a minimal form that most philosophers would agree applies at the very least to a wide range of different speech acts, and maybe to all or nearly all. Put crudely, this minimal condition on uptake says that in order for you to pull off a speech act when you produce a form of words that would customarily be associated with that act type, your audience has to understand what you are saying (which ordinarily would entail being awake, attentive, and so on).

Austin uses the example of the speech act of warning to show how this minimal formulation of the uptake requirement works. Suppose you are at a popular tourist destination, a beautiful waterfall at the top of a large cliff. You see some foreign tourists, speaking a language you do not recognize or understand, posing for photographs at the edge of the river at the top of the waterfall. You know the current is strong, the rocks slippery, and that every year, people die after being pulled over the falls. You shout, in English, 'Come back over here! I (hereby) warn you that you're in grave danger!'

Now suppose that the tourists do not know English and either have no idea that you are addressing them or think you're shouting welcoming words or encouragement. If something terrible were to happen in such a case, Austin says you could not properly say you had warned them of the danger. You might say that you had tried to warn them or that you shouted words you would use to warn an English speaker, but if they don't understand you, many people will have the intuition that no warning is made. 'If only there had been a way to warn them!' you might lament, after the events.

In this case, the question of whether the uptake requirement is met turns on whether or not the audience in fact understood the warning; if they had understood, it would be clear that the warning was made, whether the people in question eventually decided to heed it or not. Formulations of the uptake requirement that involve the actual audience reaction, though, have seemed to some philosophers to give too little power to speakers. Suppose, for example, that we are in a town hall, and a proposal is put forward that says that before a new road is built in town, a human sacrifice will be made unless someone objects. The person leading the town hall knows that there are likely to be objections, so they put cotton in their ears and wear ear muffs over the cotton just before reading the proposal and opening the objection period.

In a case like this, many people will have the intuition that someone who shouts 'I object!' should count as having objected, even if the relevant audience (the leader of the meeting) didn't hear them. (If your intuitions are affected by the fact that others in the audience might hear, imagine that everyone wears sound blocking apparatus or that there is only one person in the audience.) This intuition is bolstered by the fact that the audience's uptake failure is a culpable one – the leader took active measures to avoid having to hear possible objections.

In between this case and the original case of the language gap, we can imagine a wide range of intermediate cases. Maybe you are addressing a person that you have good reasons to think will understand you, but they happen not to; they had just been speaking English a moment ago on the phone, so you thought they knew the language, but it turns out those were lines they'd memorized for a play. Should the fact that you had good grounds to think they'd understand count for something, where the speech acts you might aim to perform are concerned? Or maybe you are addressing a person who would in fact understand you if circumstances outside of either of your control were slightly different; you share a language, are within ordinary earshot, using no fancy words or odd pronunciations, but the wind picked up and they simply didn't hear. Some philosophers have given reasons for thinking that we should count the utterances produced in these circumstances as meeting the uptake condition, even though actual uptake was not secured.

We don't have to – and won't attempt to – settle debates about exactly what kinds of uptake are required for what kinds of speech acts here in order to appreciate that there is in general a role for the requirement to play in our construction of a theory of speech acts. Regardless of where your intuitions come down with regard to the examples we have looked at so far here, that is, it seems clear that in many cases, changing the facts about uptake changes people's intuitions about whether a speech act has been realized. Furthermore, as we saw with the background and procedural requirements, there seems to be interesting variation over different speech act types with regard to what *kinds* of uptake have to be secured.

Consider Austin's example of making a bet, for example – this is an action that clearly requires more than simply that the audience understand the speaker's utterance. In order for a bet to be placed, there must be another person around, and they must agree to take the bet. While you can say 'I'll bet you sixpence it'll rain tomorrow' to a crowd of sharp-eared colinguals in a silent room, that is, if no one says 'Done!' then no bet is made. A random passer-by who happened to hear your utterance cannot track you down the following day and demand sixpence if it should turn out to be dry.

What do you think about other speech acts? What kind of uptake is required when you say 'I promise that….' Does the person to whom the promise is made have to hear you? Accept the promise? How about the naming of ships? Would a ship come to be named 'Boaty McBoatface' if the Queen broke a bottle on its bow and declared it so-named, even if there were no one around to hear?

5.3.4 NON-FATAL ERRORS

When the background, procedural, or uptake conditions aren't met, an utterance that would ordinarily realize a certain speech act will fail to do so. As we saw above, Austin calls the failures that occur in such cases 'infelicities'. In addition to these *sine qua non* requirements, he takes the felicity conditions that are associated with different speech acts to specify conditions that the best instances – the instances that maximally live up to what we expect from the action types in question – will have, but which might not always be quite completely satisfied.

Although these less serious infelicities won't be a major focus for us going forward, it's worth taking a quick look at them so that our understanding of Austin's notion of felicity conditions is complete. Most of the examples he gives of non-fatal infelicities involve the violation of what he calls conditions of sincerity:

> A good many… verbal procedures are designed for use by people who hold certain beliefs or have certain feelings or intentions. And if you use one of these formulae when you do not have the requisite thoughts or feelings or intentions then there is an abuse of the procedure, there is insincerity. Take, for example, the expression, 'I congratulate you'. This is designed for use by people who are glad that the person addressed has achieved a certain feat, believe that he was personally responsible for the success, and so on. If I say 'I congratulate you' when I'm not pleased or when I don't believe that the credit was yours, then there is insincerity. Likewise if I say I promise to do something, without having the least intention of doing it or without believing it feasible. In these cases there is something wrong, certainly, but it is not like a misfire. We should not say that I didn't in fact promise, but rather that I did promise but promised insincerely; I did congratulate you but the congratulations were hollow.
> (Austin 1962, 238-9)

To bring out the difference between this sort of failure and the sorts we looked at above, think of what exactly you reproach someone for if you learn that they aren't the least bit sorry although they apologize. Suppose someone says 'Congratulations!' but inside wishes that you hadn't succeeded at whatever it was. In many cases, we wouldn't have access to information about what people really think. But suppose they left a diary, and we somehow ended up coming across the page dealing with the day on which they congratulate you. It might read 'I congratulated the author of the winning article, although resenting them the whole time and thinking the article was bad'. This seems like a perfectly natural first-person report – the author themselves says they've congratulated the person they didn't think deserved it! Once you find this page, too, you may think 'Hm, that wasn't very nice to congratulate someone when you didn't think they deserved it.' But that response wouldn't make sense if sincerity were a condition on the performance of the speech act of congratulating in the first place. So, it's better to treat it as something we ordinarily expect, or which is conventionally associated with the act type, but not something strictly required.

5.4   A TAXONOMY OF SPEECH ACTS

As our discussion of the various ways in which a speech act or an attempted speech act may succumb to infelicity shows, different speech acts have different felicity conditions: the background require- ments they impose can vary, as do the procedures used to realize them and the degree of strictness with which those procedures must be followed, and the forms of uptake they demand.

This kind of variation opens up the interesting possibility that there could be a science of speech acts – a principled way of classifying them according to the traits they have in common. In fact, some philoso- phers have developed theories along these lines, taking there to be common clusters of properties we can use to group speech acts, and taking this fact to reveal interesting things about our cognition, our social relationships, language, and the connections between them.

Although we won't really look at that project in great detail here, it'll be worth taking a moment to point out a few of the other fea- tures, in addition to felicity conditions, that philosophers have used to categorize speech acts. The first thing to call attention to is that in the philosophical literature, the term 'speech act' is used in the way we have been using it so far in this chapter, to pick out just one of the kinds of actions you might think someone performs when they speak. But Austin, as well as many philosophers following his lead, in fact distinguishes three kinds of speech-related actions:

- Locutionary action: uttering certain words, for example, 'Shoot him!'
- Illocutionary action: performing a certain speech act, for example, ordering someone to shoot
- Perlocutionary action: causing someone to be shot

A **locutionary action** is the production of a linguistic token, like the utterance of a word or sentence. Suppose – to invoke a kind of example we have seen a few times, and will see a few more – that you are trying to learn a new language or memorize lines for a play. You utter the sentence 'Will no one rid me of this troublesome priest?' But you don't, simply in virtue of uttering the sentence, count as having asked a question, or as having issued a (veiled) command – you're just uttering the words, without intending them to amount to a speech act in the sense we've been looking at here so far.

That fuller sense of action, in the terms of our standard trifecta, is called **illocutionary action**. Illocutionary actions are all of the kinds of actions we have looked at in this chapter so far – things like promising, apologizing, declaring, and so on. The relationship between locutionary actions and illocutionary actions is an interesting one in several ways. As we have seen here, every token illocutionary action – like Char's promising on Tuesday at 7pm to come to the party the next day – is realized by some token locutionary action or other – like their producing, at that time, the words 'I promise to come to the party tomorrow'.

But, as our sentence 'Will no one rid me of this troublesome priest?' brings out the relationship between illocutionary action types and locutionary action types is not a one-to-one mapping. Depending on who is asking, the very same locutionary act might count as a request or as a demand. This flexibility runs the other way, too: the same type of illocutionary action can generally be realized by a wide variety of locutionary action types. So, you can refuse another piece of pie by saying 'No, thanks!' or 'I'm stuffed!' or 'It was lovely, but I have to drive home', and so on.

In addition to these two types of interrelated actions, it is important that we take care to distinguish the effects of an action from the action itself. Suppose, for example, that you perform the locutionary act of producing the sentence 'I couldn't eat another thing, I'm absolutely stuffed!' and in so doing, the illocutionary act of refusing another portion. Your refusal might lead to different consequences. In some contexts, the host might be very happy, as it'll mean they have a portion left over to eat tomorrow. In others, they might be offended, as they'll think it means you didn't like the food or that you're judging their ability to afford to feed you more, or whatever.

Austin called knock-on effects like these **perlocutionary actions**, although it is now common to call them **perlocutionary effects**. It is important to note that not just any effects of any action someone performs count as perlocutionary. The term's place in our trifecta is meant to reflect that it applies only to those consequences that follow from an illocutionary action someone performs. So, to take an example that is inexplicably common in the literature, you might utter the words 'Shoot him' (locutionary action), thereby giving an order (illocutionary action), and causing someone to shoot someone (perlocutionary effect). On the other hand, you might decide your subordinates aren't that reliable and just pull the trigger yourself. In this case, the resulting physical scenario would be the same, but we wouldn't talk about any perlocutionary effects.

Another dimension along which speech acts are traditionally analyzed involves a distinction between two features called **force** (sometimes 'illocutionary force') and **content**. To see what these two components amount to, consider the following examples involving **propositional attitudes**:

(24)   I believe that it will rain tomorrow.

(25)   I am afraid that it will rain tomorrow.

(26)   I hope that it will rain tomorrow.

These sentences, for our purposes, are not importantly different in terms of the speech acts they can be used to realize – they all involve statements of fact – and would typically be used to make assertions. However, they illustrate something that is interesting for us – they involve three different attitudes that a person might take toward the same proposition. The proposition in question is the proposition that it will rain tomorrow, and the attitudes are belief, fear, and hope. At the level of the entire sentence, different contents are encoded – the first encodes the content that some person believes that it will rain, the second that they fear it will, and the third that they hope it will. But at the level of the proposition the speaker takes an attitude toward, we can appreciate a sense in which the contents involved are the same in each case.

Now consider the following related phenomenon:

(27)   Kit is leaving.

(28)   Is Kit leaving?

(29)   Leave, Kit!

These sentences are different from our first three in that they don't involve propositional attitudes and in that they each involve a different kind of speech act. Like our first three, however, there is intuitively a common element shared across them – they all invoke Kit's leaving. In speech act theoretic terms, these three sentences share a content but differ in illocutionary force; the first sentence is used to make an assertion concerning Kit's leaving, the second a question about whether Kit is leaving, and the third an order that Kit leave.

Many philosophers have taken this kind of modularity – the fact that you can construct different speech acts by 'mixing and matching' forces and contents, so to speak – to be an important property of language in general and of speech acts specifically, and some linguists and philosophers think that all sentences come with overt or covert tags that indicate their illocutionary force. In these examples, for example, the distinctive question and command syntax and pronunciation might be treated as a force marker.

> Take one of the examples presented earlier from Austin. Can you use it to generate more examples, keeping the content the same and switching only the force? How about switching contents but keeping the force the same?

Another concept that is useful to have when thinking about speech acts is something called 'direction of fit'. Here, too, an example will help to bring the idea out. Imagine you find a scrap of paper with the following words written on it:

Flour, sugar, salt, milk, butter, eggs

If you see only the words, but don't know anything about the context in which they were produced, it is impossible to say for sure what speech act they would have amounted to. Elizabeth Anscombe, to whom the example is due, pointed out that words like these could be the result of at least two very different processes. On the one hand, they might constitute a shopping list, made by a forgetful person who wanted to bake a cake and needed a reminder about which ingredients should be put into their cart. On the other hand, they might come from the pages of a spy's notebook, jotted down as during a discreet mission following a shopper through the supermarket.

In terms popularized by John Searle, if the words in question form a shopping list, we might say the speech act constituted when they are written down has the 'word-to-world' direction of fit. That speech act is supposed to lay down a marker that agents should or must try to make the world match. In the spy case, Searle would say that the notes have the opposite direction of fit, 'world to word'. There, the world, as it were, lays down a marker that the person producing the words tries to meet.

It isn't totally clear that all speech acts have a direction of fit; think of exclamations like 'Oh, no!' or 'Ouch!'. While expressions like these respond to the world, in the sense of typically being produced as the result of some unfortunate or unpleasant circumstances, it isn't clear that they aim to fit in the way that a statement of fact does. Nevertheless, since many speech acts do seem to have a quite clear direction of fit, philosophers have found the notion useful as a device for categorization.

5.5 WRAPPING UP

In this chapter, following Austin, we began by drawing a distinction between sentences that are used to report on matters of fact, and sentences that are used to perform actions. In particular, we saw how a wide range of sentences that have the same basic grammatical structure as fact-reporting sentences seem to be neither true or false, despite being clearly intelligible. While you might reply to someone saying 'I (hereby) protest!' for example, or 'I (hereby) promise' by saying 'I don't care' or 'You're in no position to promise', it seems inappropriate to reply with 'That's false!'.

Austin's explanation of this fact relied on the idea that the sentences in question are distinctively performative – by uttering one, a speaker doesn't say how the world is, they perform a kind of action. We saw how instead of truth conditions, Austin takes performatives to have felicity conditions, and we looked at some of the ways in which those conditions can fail to be met.

As famous as Austin is for distinguishing constatives – his term for ordinary fact-reportings – from performatives, he is also famous for ending his book by undermining the distinction. We already noticed one area in which the distinction seems to blur in our discussion above; we saw how you can take any fact-reporting sentence and make it into a kind of performative by saying 'I hereby assert that…' to the beginning of it. Austin points out an example in which a farmer puts a sign in a field that says 'Dangerous bull'. Is this a state-ment or a warning? It seems like there are reasons to think that it could be taken either way – if there is no bull in the field or the bull is not dangerous, then what the sign says seems false. But on the other hand, it seems clear that the point of the sign is to warn people – if someone should meet an unwelcome fate in the field, the farmer's lawyers would surely point out that the farmer had warned passers-by.

Austin's response to tricky cases like these, which we will assume for the rest of Part Two, is that constativity and performativity come in degrees and are typically intermingled with one another. Every time we make a statement, there is a clear sense in which we are performing an action – when you say 'It is raining' you aren't merely holding the proposition that it is raining up for people to see in an abstract way in the way you might if you were to say 'Imagine for a moment that it were raining…', but are rather taking on a certain sort of commitment to the truth of the proposition. That much already falls out of the picture of communication we developed in Part One, the bits about truth and trust. To put the same point in a slightly different way, reporting a fact is performing a kind of action.

But there is still something important to be gained from noting that the class of actions we realize in speaking goes beyond the reporting of facts. Even if there is a sense in which some of the more performative things we do might have echoes of truth conditionality – imagine a police officer that says 'You're under arrest', but who didn't notice that they were standing just outside the county in which they have jurisdiction. You might say 'Unfortunately for you, I'm not. Look where you're standing!' as you laugh and jump into your getaway car. There is still, nevertheless, as we will see in the chapters to come, much to be gained from noticing that we can also change the facts by speaking, in the way we do when we say 'I swear (the oath of office)', 'I promise...', 'I bet you that...', and so on.

FURTHER READING

Key sources for the material presented in this chapter include:

- J.L. Austin. *How to Do Things with Words*. Harvard University Press, 1962.

For readers who want to explore related topics in greater detail, I recommend:

- Green, Mitchell, "Speech Acts", The Stanford Encyclopedia of Philosophy (Fall 2021 Edition), Edward N. Zalta (ed.)
- John Searle. *Speech Acts*. Cambridge University Press, 1969.

SILENCING, DISABLING, AND DISTORTION

Warning

The discussion in this chapter will involve disturbing topics of a sexual nature. The second paragraph of the chapter includes a quotation describing a particularly upsetting form of pornography involving depictions of rape, and frequent reference in general terms to non-consensual sex will be made throughout the chapter.

6.1 LANGTON/HORNSBY – PORNOGRAPHY AS SPEECH

Anyone who has used the internet will at some point likely have encountered pornography in one form or another – even with content blockers, age controls, and in some locations, government restrictions, a combination of the basic structure of the network and strong financial incentives makes content that ordinary people would characterize as pornographic hard to remain unaware of. In earlier times, however, things were different; until relatively recently, people who wanted to consume pornography would have had to make some effort to seek out photographs, magazines, or films, or pay to view

DOI: 10.4324/9781003250753-6

them. The nature of the channels for distribution made (somewhat) effective controls on access feasible, and for a long time pornography was prohibited in many jurisdictions. From 1873 in the United States, for example, the so-called 'Comstock laws' made it illegal to send basically any description or depiction of anything remotely involving sex in the mail. By the 1960s, however, prohibitions on the distribution and consumption of pornography began to fall apart. While US courts have consistently found that the First Amendment does not guarantee people the right to produce or distribute obscene material, difficulties in precisely characterizing obscenity in a plausible way have led to a situation in which even depictions of women

> dehumanized as sexual objects, things or commodities; enjoying pain or humiliation or rape; being tied up, cut up, mutilated, bruised, or physically hurt; in postures of sexual submission or servility or display; reduced to body parts, penetrated by objects or animals, or presented in scenarios of degradation, injury, torture; shown as filthy or inferior; bleeding, bruised or hurt in a context which makes these conditions sexual.
> (MacKinnon 1987, 176, quoted in Langton 1993, 293-4)

have been classified as protected speech. Even judges and legislatures who take such depictions to harm women, leading to 'affront and lower pay at work, insult and injury at home, battery and rape on the streets' (American Booksellers, Inc. v. Hudnut, quoted in Langton 1993, 294) have concluded that antipornography legislation would run afoul of the First Amendment. In many cases, courts have found that pornographers' free speech rights trump women's claims about the harms pornography causes.

Both in collaboration and independently during the 1990s and early 2000s, philosophers Rae Langton and Jennifer Hornsby, drawing on some work of Catherine MacKinnon's (a law professor who in fact helped draft legislation on the subject), developed a line of reasoning in response to these findings that has led to the development of a large and influential philosophical literature. Our focus for the rest of this chapter will be on two early arguments from Langton, and on a pair of related proposals that have emerged in the years since.

The first of Langton's arguments invokes women's right to equal protection under the 14th Amendment; by placing women in a subordinate position to men, the argument claims, pornography violates

women's constitutional right to equality. The second argument inge-
niously meets a First Amendment claim with a First Amendment
claim; according to it, the kind of speech that is at issue where
pornography is concerned can be justifiably infringed, not because
it involves bad outcomes for women in general, but because it *itself*
infringes on women's constitutionally protected right to speech. As
we shall see below, Langton's claim is that pornography literally makes
it the case that there are things women cannot do in speaking, things
that they have a clear interest in being able to do and which they
would be able to do if not for their gender.

6.1.1 PORNOGRAPHY SUBORDINATES WOMEN

Recall the distinction we drew in Chapter Five between locutionary
actions, illocutionary actions, and their perlocutionary effects:

- Locutionary action: uttering certain words, for example, 'Shoot
  him!'
- Illocutionary action: performing a certain speech act, for example,
  ordering someone to shoot
- Perlocutionary effects: someone's being shot

With this set of distinctions in mind, let us look at some of the ways in
which speech might involve **subordination** – one person or group's
being placed lower than another somehow in a social hierarchy. It is
not difficult to see that subordination can be a perlocutionary effect
of speech. Suppose we are new recruits in a rigidly hierarchical organization, like the military or the police. Officially, our status is equal –
recruit is the lowest status. But for some reason, the drill instructor
charged with our training doesn't like me, and every day they assign
me toilet cleaning duty at the same time they assign you free recre-
ation. It seems plausible to think that in a case like this, as a *result* of
the instructor's illocutions, I end up subordinate to you in important
ways. If everyone in the group sees every day that this happens to me,
they may start to afford you more respect than me, be more keen to
associate with you than me, and so on. Research in psychology suggests that even if you know the distribution of goods here is arbitrary
or worse, even positively and intentionally unfair, you are likely to
come to see yourself as superior to me after a fairly short time.

Could pornography, or at least, the particularly vile sort of material Langton describes in the passage quoted above, produce the subordination of women as a perlocutionary effect? Without taking a position on the empirical question of whether it in fact leads to subordination, it seems clear that this is a possibility that deserves to be taken seriously. It is not hard to imagine how someone who is exposed to depictions of women in servile or submissive positions, being humiliated or made to feel pain, treated as objects, and so on, but who never sees men depicted in this way might end up forming beliefs or dispositions that place women in a lower position than men.

Crucially, however, while this kind of subordination seems like a plausible outcome of exposure to pornography, this is not the sense of subordination Langton is interested in. Her idea, which she credits MacKinnon with originating, is that pornography involves not merely harmful or unwanted perlocutionary but *illocutionary* subordination, or subordination in speech act terms. It's not just that pornography *causes* people to treat women as inferior, but rather that '*in* depicting subordination, pornography subordinates' (emphasis in original, 1993, 302). To show what is distinctive about this claim, Langton presents an example involving apartheid:

> Consider this utterance: 'Blacks are not permitted to vote'. Imagine that it is uttered by a legislator in Pretoria in the context of enacting legislation that underpins apartheid. It is a locutionary act: by 'Blacks' it refers to blacks. It is a perlocutionary act: it will have the effect, among others, that blacks stay away from polling booths. But it is, first and foremost, an illocutionary act: it makes it the case that blacks are not permitted to vote. It plausibly subordinates blacks. So does this utterance: 'Whites only'. It too is a locutionary act: by 'Whites' it refers to whites. It has some important perlocutionary effects: it keeps blacks away from white areas, ensures that only whites go there, and perpetuates racism. It is – one might say – a perlocutionary act of subordination. But it is also an illocutionary act: it orders blacks away, welcomes whites, permits whites to act in a discriminatory way towards blacks. It subordinates blacks. If this is correct, then there is no sleight of hand, no philosophical impropriety, about the claim that a certain kind of speech can be an illocutionary act of subordination.
> (Langton 1993, 303)

Langton takes the illocutionary acts realized by a person in power's authoritatively saying 'Blacks are not permitted to vote' or 'Whites only' to involve three elements that constitute subordination: they *rank* people hierarchically, with Black people placed below white people, they *legitimate* discrimination, and they *deprive* Black people of power and rights that white people retain.

If we treat pornography as speech, we can ask whether it subordinates women in something like the way these racist utterances, produced by a politically-empowered figure, could realize subordinating speech acts. Although the case is more complicated than the case of the apartheid legislator, Langton thinks it is a striking intuitive fact that the vocabulary of speech acts applies so naturally to pornography. She quotes MacKinnon saying that pornography 'celebrates, promotes, authorizes and legitimates' (1993, 307) behaviors that are degrading to women and that involve abuse. It does not seem misplaced, that is, to think that by depicting men as the deserving beneficiaries of sexual pleasure and women as the means, pornography could *rank* women, placing them below men in a hierarchy. Nor does it seem like a confusion to say that the depictions in question *legitimizes* the ranking they portray, making it in a sense acceptable for men to treat women as unequal, and to inflict violence in the ways pornography depicts.

Of course, there is at least one big difference between the legislator and the pornographer. The legislator is legally empowered to change the facts, as it were, about who can vote or who can go where by speaking. The pornographer has no such legal authority. But does that mean they have no authority at all to *deprive* women of rights? Langton thinks that'd be an overly hasty conclusion. After all, many speech acts involve forms of social authority that are less rigorously codified than those that have a legal definition. You don't need support from the law to make a bet, or promise, for example, with your friends. Nevertheless, making a bet or a promise is an action you undertake that changes the social landscape in definite ways – if you fail to follow through, and your friends say 'That person isn't cool, they make promises they don't keep', you won't defuse the accusation by saying 'Yes, I made a promise, but it wasn't a legally binding one'. The social fact that we all take promises to be binding is enough to make them so.

The idea that pornographers have a similar sort of social authority is an important piece of Langton's subordination argument. While she thinks it will ultimately be an empirical question whether the audiences who consume pornography treat the pornographers as authoritative or not, she thinks it is plausible that they do in at least one domain: the domain that concerns how people do and ought to behave around sex. If it should turn out that people who consume pornography end up treating it as though it were in the business of characterizing the 'rules of the game', as it were, telling people what things to do and how to do them, and what things are ok to do, then it will turn out that there is a substantive sense in which pornography does in fact have the power to set those rules.

6.1.2   PORNOGRAPHY SILENCES WOMEN

Langton's second argument in favor of restrictions on pornography is an argument that sets pornographers' alleged right to expression against women's right to the same. In brief, Langton alleges that there is a sense in which pornography undermines women's speech, and indeed, undermines a particularly important form of speech.

To see what this sense amounts to, consider some of the ways in which one person might prevent another from speaking. To invoke our locution–illocution–perlocution distinction again, it's clear that one way to silence someone would be by undermining their locutionary abilities, that is, by preventing them from producing words in the first place. Langton provides examples in which a certain population is intimidated by someone threatening bad consequences if they speak. If I credibly tell you, for example, that if you utter any words for the next hour, I'll fail you in my course, and my course matters for your future, then by producing that threat I can silence you with regard to your locutionary activity. I could locutionarily silence even more directly by putting tape over your mouth, and perhaps less directly by creating an environment in which there is nothing straightforwardly preventing you from speaking, but in which you have the expectation that it would be pointless to speak because no one would listen, or in which you generally fear the consequences of speaking up (as in politically responsive self-censorship).

This last scenario – the creation of a generally hostile environment – points toward a second way in which someone might silence someone else: by undercutting the perlocutionary effects their speech produces. Suppose, for example, that we are members of a mean club, which lets in some members just so that the other members have someone to be rude toward or dismissive to. You join the club, hoping to make friends and go to the fun parties our club is known for hosting, but unfortunately for you, you're one of the people we let in just to be mean to.

One of the ways in which we play our mean game is that we direct all the other members, and all of the people who work in our mean clubhouse, to ignore you whenever you ask for drinks, invite someone to dance, and so on. You show up at the first party, someone says in a welcoming tone, 'Can I get you a drink?'. You reply, 'No alcohol for me, thanks, but could I have a seltzer water?' and they just pretend they didn't hear you. You say again 'How about a seltzer?' and they continue ignoring you. In this case, everyone in the vicinity hears what you've said (your locutionary act is recognized) and understands that you're asking for a seltzer water (so the force and content of the illocution involved are recognized), but your words fail to have the effect you aimed for (i.e., getting a seltzer).

Finally, we can imagine cases in which someone utters words – realizes a locutionary act – but in which those words fail to count as the kind of illocution they would have counted as in someone else's mouth, or in some other context. As our discussion from Chapter Five made clear, there are three general sorts of ways in which an attempted illocutionary act can go fatally wrong – by failure of the background, performance, or uptake conditions.

To take an example Austin gives of what in our terms would count as a *background condition* failure, if some 'low type' (his words) should snatch the bottle of champagne from the Queen's hand just as she was about to christen a ship, saying 'I hereby name this ship the Generalissimo Stalin', the event will not count as a christening. Of course, the ship does not end up named the Stalin (no perlocutionary effect) – but even more fundamentally, the speech act of christening isn't realized to begin with: only the monarch can perform christenings!

In Chapter Five, we illustrated the possibility of a procedural failure by looking at examples of oath-taking, including a particularly poignant case involving pro-democracy activists who had won elections to the Hong Kong Legislative Council. If the procedure isn't followed exactly, as we saw, the illocutionary act might not be realized.

To illustrate how failure of uptake can undermine an attempted illocutionary act, consider an example that has played a particularly prominent role in the literature:

> An actor is acting a scene in which there is supposed to be a fire. (Albee's *Tiny Alice*, for example.) It is his role to imitate as persuasively as he can a man who is trying to warn others of a fire. 'Fire!' he screams. And perhaps he adds, at the behest of the author, 'I mean it! Look at the smoke!' etc. And now a real fire breaks out, and the actor tries vainly to warn the real audience. 'Fire!' he screams. 'I mean it! Look at the smoke!' etc.
> (Davidson 1979, 7)

In this case, which might remind you of our example from Chapter Five of the person trying to warn others about the danger of a waterfall, it seems clear that no warning is made. In both cases, this fact is due to a failure of uptake – in order for some words to count as a warning, the audience has to take them to be a warning. Unlike our waterfall example, the problem here isn't that the audience doesn't know the language of the speaker. In the theater, the problem is due to the structure of audience expectations as they relate to the author's locutionary actions – since he's taken to be acting, he can't 'break through' as it were, and realize the speech acts an arbitrary member of the public would be able to. In Langton's terms, this results in his being illocutionarily silenced.

In summary, then, we have three ways in which a person might be silenced, that is, undermined as a speaker. They might be prevented from realizing locutionary acts, their speech might be deprived of its ordinary or expected perlocutionary effects, or they might be prevented from performing illocutionary actions.

The heart of Langton's second argument about pornography is the claim that it **illocutionarily silences** women by undermining the uptake conditions for certain speech acts that all people have an interest in being able to realize. In particular, Langton claims that pornography can prevent women from being able to use their speech to refuse sex; a woman might say 'no', intending to refuse, but fail to count as refusing in virtue of her words' not securing uptake. In this circumstance, she finds herself in a position somewhat like Davidson's actor – but the role is not one she can step out of after the play is over.

Where the act of refusing sex is concerned, in Langton's terms:

> The felicity conditions for women's speech acts are set by the speech acts of pornography. The words of the pornographer, like the words of the legislator, are 'words that set conditions'. They are words that constrain, that make certain action – refusal, protest – unspeakable for women in some contexts. This is speech that determines the kind of speech there can be.
> (Langton 1993, 324)

Think about the scenario we touched on above, in which people – in particular, men and boys – treat pornographers' depictions as authoritative in terms of setting the rules of the game. Again, while this argument will ultimately have to rest on empirical premises, It isn't difficult to imagine that repeated exposure to scenes in which women are depicted in sexualized submissive roles, enjoying 'pain or humiliation or rape' (Langton 1993: 293) could lead to circumstances in which the prevailing norms are terrible for women. Again, in Langton's terms:

> Pornography … may simply leave no space for the refusal move in its depictions of sex. In pornography of this kind there would be all kinds of locutions the women depicted could use to make the consent move. 'Yes' is one such locution. 'No' is just another. Here the refusal move is not itself eroticized … it is absent altogether. Consent is the only thing a woman can do with her words in this game. Someone learning the rules of the game from this kind of pornography might not even recognize an attempted refusal. 'Coming from her, I took it as consent', he might say. Refusal would be made unspeakable for a woman in that context.
> (Langton 1993, 324)

6.2   MAITRA – SILENCING RECONCEIVED AS COMMUNICATIVE DISABLEMENT

Ishani Maitra has developed an influential alternative characterization of silencing that builds on some of the basic insights from Langton and Hornsby but deviates from their model in several important regards that it will be worth our time to consider here. While Maitra agrees that Langton and Hornsby have identified an important phenomenon, she thinks the details of their proposal expose it to some challenges, and she takes the notion of silencing that results to be less general than it could and ought to be. Maitra's own account of silencing aims to avoid those challenges, while showing how silencing is a theoretical tool that can help us understand a range of intuitive injustices that go beyond those involved in pornography.

The central issue Maitra takes Langton and Hornsby's account to run into is illustrated by means of an example originally proposed by Daniel Jacobson. Jacobson agrees with Langton and Hornsby that if pornography undermines women's ability to refuse sex, that amounts to a very serious problem.

But, Jacobson points out, not all cases of illocutionary disempowerment are problematic. In fact, sometimes it even seems like a *good* thing when certain peoples' speech ends up failing to count as the realization of a speech act. Children, for example, can produce whatever words they like, but those words will never amount to actions that allow them to get married or enter into other legally binding agreements. Far from denouncing this as a form of silencing, though, most people will agree this is as it should be! This raises the question: when is it ok for someone's illocutionary range to be limited, and when is it not?

Jacobson himself suggests that we should explain the difference between cases in which silencing is acceptable or good and cases in which it is not in terms of the *effects* that result from it. Since everyone agrees that it is bad for children to be married or entangled in contractual obligations, limiting their power to put themselves in such situations is good. On the other hand, Jacobson says, if women are unable to refuse sex, very bad outcomes occur:

> What is so terrible about a woman's being unable to refuse sex is the disablement of her autonomy, the resulting violation of her body, and assault on her well-being.
> (Jacobson 1995, 76)

Langton and Hornsby will of course agree that any case in which a woman's autonomy and bodily integrity are violated as a result of systematic illocutionary disablement involves something terrible. They cannot, however, agree with Jacobson that this is *the* thing that makes silencing bad – the defining thing – without losing a part of the argument that was important to them. Their aim, recall, was to respond to pornographers' claim to protection under the First Amendment to the US Constitution by pointing out a way in which pornography *itself* infringes women's right to speech.

As many commentators have pointed out in this literature and elsewhere, however, the right to free speech does not plausibly extend to cover the *effects* that speech has; while the First Amendment guarantees your right to stand in the street with a placard that says 'Repent! The end is nigh!', it does not guarantee you the right to actually make people repent or believe that the end is nigh. Similarly, the right to say 'Stop!' is plausibly protected, as the right to refuse might be, but anything beyond that – like actually stopping someone, or *successfully* refusing (in the sense of achieving certain perlocutionary outcomes) – will fall outside the scope of free speech protections.

Maitra takes this to show that we need a way of carving up the set of illocutionary actions into those that deserve protection and those that don't. We need a way, that is, to explain why women should have the inalienable right to perform the illocutionary act of refusal, but children should not have a similar right to perform the illocutionary act of getting married. But we need to offer an explanation that doesn't depend on reference to the effects that follow after either act. Once we let the effects that result from a speech act into our evaluation of it, she thinks, Maitra thinks, we aren't really evaluating the act on its own terms as speech.

Maitra proposes to make this division by identifying a special class of speech acts she calls **communicative acts**. In order to characterize acts of this sort, she relies on Grice's notion of speaker meaning, which we saw in Chapter Three but reproduce here:

> A speaker *S* means something by uttering *x* iff, for some audience *A*, *S* utters *x* intending:
> (i) *A* to produce a response *r*;
> (ii) *A* to think (recognize) that *S* intends (i); and,
> (iii) *A*'s fulfillment of (ii) to give him a reason to fulfill (i)
> (Grice 1989, 92)

When we introduced this template previously, we were trying to answer the question of where linguistic meanings come from. Grice's answer, in a nutshell, was that an expression means what it is used to communicate – to get across to someone. Maitra thinks we can employ a Gricean notion of communication, without worrying too much about what meaning a certain speech act encodes. Consider the following passage, in which by 'informative intention' she means Grice's condition (i) and by 'communicative intention', she means Grice's (ii).

> As a first pass, we might say that a communicative act is successful iff the speaker has the intentions required by the Gricean account, and the intended audience satisfies those intentions. But in fact, this requires too much. Consider … Amy's refusing Ben's offer of coffee. Suppose that Ben thinks Amy is a habitual liar. Then, even upon hearing her refusal, he may not come to believe that she doesn't want the cup of coffee, all things considered. So, Amy's informative intention isn't satisfied. Nevertheless, intuitively Amy has succeeded in communicating her refusal. That is to say, her communicative act has succeeded. Accordingly, satisfaction of the first intention, i.e., the informative intention, is not necessary for successful communication. Satisfaction of the other two intentions is both necessary and sufficient for full success of a communicative act.
> (Maitra 2009, 327)

The key thing to notice here is that for Maitra, you can say 'I don't want coffee' and thereby communicate that you don't want coffee without it actually being the case that the person you're talking to comes to believe that you don't want coffee. One way to put this point might be to say that there is a sense in which communicative speech acts are indifferent to (some of) the actual effects they produce. On Maitra's Gricean model, I want to produce a response, R, when I say something. But whether I succeed in communicating or not doesn't depend on whether R is produced, it depends rather on whether my audience sees that I wanted that response to be produced. (In Maitra's official terms, communicative acts are indifferent to whether the speaker's informative intention is met; the communicative intention and its reflexive counterpart are what determine whether the act was realized.)

Armed with this notion of communication, Maitra thinks we can distinguish the kinds of illocutionary actions that are plausibly protected by our right to free speech from the kind that are not. The ones that are protected, she thinks, are precisely the communicative ones, that is, the ones that require just that someone see what you're up to when you make an attempt. The kinds of actions that are not protected are the ones that require more substantial forms of uptake – that is, the ones that will satisfy a speaker only when they bring some substantive effects along with them.

As examples of communicative acts, Maitra mentions warning, criticism, and protest. Intuitively, these all seem like act types that I succeed in performing simply by getting you to see *that* they are the acts I am attempting to perform. To reprise our example of a warning shouted to people at the edge of a dangerous river above a waterfall, imagine that instead of thinking that you were encouraging them to dive in (as we said when we introduced the example), they saw that you aimed to warn them. In this case, it would seem fair to say that you did warn them, even if they don't share a language with you. If they understood that your gestures and shouts were meant to get them to recognize a danger, then whether they heed your warning or not, it seems fair for you to say later at the inquest 'I did warn them before it all happened'.

This consequence-independent property of communicative acts stands in contrast to the situation we find when we consider illocutionary actions like offending, comforting, placating, and so on. In a charming example, Grice himself suggests that if a person should cut in front of him in the street, whether it is an insult or not depends on whether or not the person *intended* that he see it as one. In order for me to count as offending you, on the other hand, more than just a recognition of my intention is required – I actually have to make it the case that you feel a certain way. In other words, you can insult me without my caring, but you only offend me if I care.

Maitra could allow failures of uptake that occur in non-communicative cases to count as a form of injustice. For example, if women could never make amends by apologizing because men never forgive them, that seems like it would be an intuitively unjust state of affairs. But her goal is to develop an alternative to Langton and Hornsby's model of silencing that focuses on communicative acts:

> On my view, a speaker is **communicatively disabled** iff she is unable to fully successfully perform her intended communicative act, because her intended audience fails to satisfy either the second or the third of her (Gricean) intentions.
> (Maitra 2009, 327-328, bold added)

What can Maitra's communicative disablement do that Langton and Hornsby's notion of illocutionary silencing cannot? One advantage it offers is that it suggests a way to solve the problem we started with: how to explain the intuition that it's ok when children's words fail to count as constituting a marriage, but not when women's words fail to count as a refusal. While the consequences of the two cases were obviously different, we wanted an explanation that could differentiate them without invoking those consequences.

Now Maitra has given us the outline of such an explanation: we don't have a free speech right to marry, since getting married isn't a communicative act. So if someone's right to marry by saying some words is infringed, whether that's a problem or not depends on the other rights they have. Since children don't have the right to marry, the fact that their words fail to produce that effect is not morally problematic. Refusing, on the other hand, is a communicative act. To succeed in making a refusal, it's enough that someone sees that that's what you intend to do by way of a certain expression. So, if someone is unable to realize this kind of action, that amounts to a free speech infringement. (Of course, you might wonder – why are communicative actions protected in a way that others are not? That question is too big for us here, but one thing Maitra says is that speech is unique in that it is cheap and in principle available to everyone.)

At the same time, Maitra thinks her notion of communicative disablement can explain the things Langton and Hornsby's original take on silencing did. To look at their central case, is not difficult to imagine circumstances in which women could be communicatively disabled in ways that would undermine their ability to refuse sex. Here is an example Maitra gives involving that situation:

> Scenario 1: A woman says 'No' to a man, intending to refuse sex. The man understands the conventional meaning of her utterance, and recognizes the content it expresses. Nevertheless, the utterance does not do what she wants it to do: it does not deter him from forcing sex on her.
> (Maitra 2009, 313)

One of the ways in which this scenario might be brought about could be if the man fails to recognize the woman's communicative intention. While Maitra isn't specifically focused on the case of pornography, the kind of environment Langton and Hornsby describe, where people who consume pornography end up with the impression that it is an accurate portrayal of 'how the game of sex is played', provides a suggestion about how a man might end up going wrong in this way.

By depicting men as the deserving beneficiaries of sexual pleasure and women as the means, as we suggested it might do earlier, pornography could lead men to end up thinking of women merely as sexual objects, whose desires and intentions simply aren't relevant in a sexual context. Or a man might think of a woman as someone with her own desires and intentions, but for whom all moves are 'yes' moves. He might think, that is, that her intention in saying 'No' is for him to see her as inviting him into a certain kind of role-play or to be expressing her desire to be seen as coy. Either interpretation would make it the case that her 'No' not count as a refusal in Maitra's terms, since her communicative intention would be unrecognized.

In addition to the fact that it fits the original cases that were in focus in the silencing literature, Maitra points out that her notion of communicative disablement allows us to explain some other phenomena that are intuitively important. In particular, she thinks her theory does a good job addressing the moral differences between various ways in which people's communicative intentions can be frustrated or undermined by the circumstances they happen to find themselves in. To see this, consider two scenarios Maitra describes:

> Scenario 2: At a dinner party, the hostess presses a guest to help himself to more food. The guest is already full, and does not want any more. So he refuses the further helping. His hostess understands the conventional meaning of his utterance. But she also supposes that he is simply being polite, not wanting to appear too greedy. She supposes that good guests always say

something similar when offered more food. As a result, she disregards his protests, and continues to press food on him, until he finally feels that he must give in.

Scenario 3: In a philosophy class, an African-American student offers a counter-example to a proposal the class is considering. The teacher understands the conventional meaning of his utterance. But given her beliefs about African-American students in general, she has low expectations of this student. In particular, she thinks that African-American students tend not to understand how philosophical arguments work. Accordingly, she fails to recognize his intention to offer a counter-example, and instead, re-explains the proposal to him. Later in the class, a white student re-states the same counter-example, and the teacher recognizes that it devastates the proposal.
(Maitra 2009, 333)

Both Scenario 2 and Scenario 3 involve communicative disablement – the speaker's communicative intentions are not recognized, and the speech acts they wanted to perform fail to count. Maitra calls readers' attention to several important differences, however, which can help us to understand the intuition that Scenario 3 is intuitively morally more upsetting than Scenario 2. Of course, the fact that the speaker in Scenario 2 ends up with his desires frustrated only as regards an additional serving of food is part of the story. Being forced into sex or undermined in the way the student in Scenario 3 is obviously worse than having more pea soup or pumpkin pie handed to you.

But there are other important factors at play here, too, which we would do well to notice. The first is that the *reasons* the people who are communicatively disabled in Scenario 2 and Scenario 3 are different. In Scenario 2, the person's communicative intention goes unrecognized because of their status as a guest at a dinner party, a circumstance in which it's common for people to politely decline food that they in fact would like to have. In Scenario 3, the speaker is communicatively disabled as a result of the way they are racialized.

Maitra thinks there is an important difference between communicative disablement that results from a temporary social identity, which all of us will occupy at different times and which we easily slip in and out of, as opposed to a stable social identity that tracks us across a wide range of contexts in our lives and which we have very little ability to change. In addition to the fact that the interpreter's mistake in Scenario 2 seems like a warranted one – since people do often in fact refuse food they want – while the interpreter's mistake in Scenario 3 is unwarranted, the *persistence* of the kind of social identity involved in Scenario 3 means that people undermined in this way are likely to face the same kind of undermining elsewhere, which seems plausibly like it produce a positive feedback loop, with each undermining contributing to the conditions under which future underminings become more likely.

6.3   KUKLA – SPEECH ACT 'QUEERING' IS DISCURSIVE INJUSTICE

The last proposal I want to survey in this chapter due to Quill Kukla, focuses on a phenomenon they call 'discursive injustice'. Like Maitra's communicative disablement, Kukla's notion of discursive injustice is intended to diagnose a problem that might show up in a wide range of contexts involving speech; while the notion can be straightforwardly applied to the question of whether pornography undermines women's attempts to refuse sex, that is just one application among many, both with regard to the type of speech act involved and with regard to the social position of the speaker. So, while Kukla focuses their discussion on 'women and … speaking from a gendered subject position' they say: 'this emphasis is to some extent arbitrary; I could have explored examples focusing on race, class, home region, or disability, for instance' (Kukla 2014, 441).

As with Langton, Hornsby, and Maitra's views, the notion of the uptake that speech acts are met with lies at the heart of Kukla's proposal. Kukla understands uptake, however, in a way that is quite distinctive when compared with the other authors we have considered. While we have already seen differences in the role uptake plays in Langton and Hornsby's work in contrast with Maitra's, there is a sense in which the two proposals we have looked at so far share a common thread: both are focused on the consequences of the fact that certain speakers in certain contexts can fail to count as having realized the speech act they intended.

While Kukla of course acknowledges that it's a big deal if words that you could reasonably expect to count as a refusal fail to count as a refusal, their understanding of the uptake conditions on speech acts opens space for us to appreciate a further set of harms you might be exposed to in cases like this. On Kukla's view, in addition to whatever is problematic about a person's not hitting the target they aimed at, we need to ask about what happens when they end up hitting *something else entirely*, that is, when they end up not only failing to do what they wanted to do, but doing something different.

To see what Kukla has in mind, consider an example they give:

> Celia is a floor manager at a heavy machinery factory where 95% of the workers are male. It is part of her job description that she has the authority to give orders to the workers on her floor, and that she should use this authority. She uses straightforward, polite locutions to tell her workers what to do: 'Please put that pile over here', 'Your break will be at 1:00 today', and so on. Her workers, however, think she is a 'bitch', and compliance is low.
> (Kukla 2014, 445)

What candidate explanations could we give for the fact that the people who work under Celia fail to consistently follow the legitimate orders she gives them on the job? Of course, one simple possibility is that the employees in question are openly sexist and just refuse to take orders from a woman. Another possibility, which Kukla thinks is both more philosophically interesting and which raises a distinctive set of ethical issues, is that background facts about the social context prevent the workers from being able to *hear* Celia's utterances as orders in the first place:

> Let's imagine ... that the workers are deeply unaccustomed to taking women as authorities in the male-dominated space of the workplace – the skills that they have mastered that govern conversation with females in the workplace simply don't include conventions for recognizing them as issuing orders and responding accordingly. Instead, they hear and respond to all of Celia's orders as requests.
> (Kukla 2014, 446)

All of the theorists we have considered so far will agree that in this case, Celia's words fail to have the status of orders; she's clearly communicatively disabled in Maitra's sense and many of the components of illocutionary silencing seem to be in place, too. The key thing that sets Kukla's view apart from Langton and Hornsby's, on the one hand, or Maitra's, on the other, concerns the *upshot* of the fact that the workers 'hear and respond to all of Celia's orders as requests' – Kukla says that in this case, in virtue of the reception they're given, Celia's words *actually count as requests*.

This is because Kukla thinks that the kind of uptake that matters for determining which speech act someone's locutionary act amounted to on a particular occasion is just whatever in fact happens in the social world, which is constituted by what people think. In their words:

> The uptake of a speech act is others' enacted recognition of its impact on social space. Intentions in speaking are part of the story that gives a speech act the performative force it has, but they are not privileged or definitive; the speaker may only discover, in how her utterance is taken up, what sort of speech act it really was.
> (Kukla 2014, 444)

While we don't have the space here to fully explore the justification that could be given for this approach to uptake, we have already seen a few examples that speak in favor of the position. Recall our discussion earlier about what it takes to count as being in a position that allows you to perform certain speech acts; in some domains, this required the legal facts to be a certain way, but in many cases, facts about whether people act as though you're in that position are what determine whether you are or not. To the best of my knowledge, there are no laws that say that 11-year-olds can't make promises. Whether an 11-year-old's uttering some words using the verb 'to promise' amounts to a binding commitment or not plausibly depends on how the social landscape is changed after the utterance is produced. If the audience are children, and the speaker says, 'I promise I will give you my juice if you hand this note to the teacher', and the other children take the speaker to be committed, then they seem to be committed. If the audience are adults, and the child says 'I promise to give you all of the money I earn forever when I'm older if you give me a soda', then no one takes the normative landscape to be changed. No new obligations are created – instead of counting as a promise, then, the child's utterance is treated as nothing more than the expression of a cute intention.

If we take seriously the possibility that the response your words elicit determines which speech act they realized, we can appreciate a new set of ways in which people can be harmed, undermined, or subject to unfairness. In particular, Kukla claims, we can appreciate how people with a disempowered social identity might have their speech act possibilities distorted in ways that further disadvantage them:

> When members of a disadvantaged group face a systematic inability to produce a specific kind of speech act that they are entitled to perform – and in particular when their attempts result in their actually producing a different kind of speech act that further compromises their social position and agency – then they are victims of what I call **discursive injustice**.
> (Kukla 2014, 440, bold added)

Think about Celia's case again – what caused her to be unable to issue orders, in a workplace environment in which a man uttering the same words she uttered would have been issuing orders was her gender identity? Her comparatively disempowered status as a woman, that is, as a person who in virtue of the way they present as gendered is taken to be less authoritative, and so on. But now think about how her inability to issue orders – and more precisely, the fact that the orders she attempts to issue end up being requests – affects her social status. As Kukla notes, requests don't meet the same degree of compliance as orders from a superior do. So her performance at work will be affected. The fact that she keeps requesting that people do things that they aren't required to do also constitutes her as a 'bitch'.

But these facts lay down new layers on top of the existing way that gender is conceptualized in the world Celia and her employees live in. The next woman to work at the factory is more likely to face the same kind of discursive injustice Celia faced, and when her speech acts result in a less empowering force than the ones she had good reason to expect to be able to perform, that fact will add yet another layer, and on and on.

Kukla points to many examples of this phenomenon, involving a female professor whose expert testimony is treated as an entreaty to be taken seriously, women whose testimony is treated as an emotional outburst (i.e., not as assertions to be taken literally), and so on.

Kukla also provides an example of a superficially similar case that they think *doesn't* amount to discursive injustice, which it'll be worth considering here in order to underscore some key features of their proposal:

> Consider an older male faculty member who is attracted to his young female graduate student. Being a basically well-intentioned fellow, what he would like to do is to invite her, in the gentlest possible terms, to reciprocate his affections. Indeed, he is horrified at the idea that she might take him as ordering or even requesting that she have sex with him; he does not want her to feel compelled to sleep with him, or even to sleep with him as the granting of a favor. He wants to sleep with her only if she is genuinely and freely interested. And so he tries to issue this invitation. But it may well be that no matter how he words and performs the speech act in accordance with the standard conventions for issuing an invitation – no matter how much he assures her that he is inviting rather than requesting or ordering, that there will be no repercussions from her turning him down, and so on – it is simply impossible for him to broach the topic without creating pressure to acquiesce.
>
> (Kukla 2014, 455)

This case has many of the key features of discursive injustice. A person, in virtue of their social identity, is prevented from realizing a speech act that the conventions associated with the form of words involved would lead them to believe they will be able to perform, and which other people would have been able to perform using those words. But Kukla says this is clearly *not* a case of discursive injustice. Why? Because it misses out a key element: the professor's failure to be able to do with his words what he wanted to and what others could have done does *is not the product of his disadvantaged position*, and it does not contribute to entrenching his disadvantage. If anything, the opposite is true – the reason the professor isn't able to pull of the kind of non-imposing request he'd like to pull off is precisely because of the powerful social position he occupies.

FURTHER READING

Key sources for the material presented in this chapter include:

- Rebecca Kukla. "Performative force, convention, and discursive injustice". In: *Hypatia* 29.2 (2014), pp. 440–457.
- Rae Langton. "Speech acts and unspeakable acts". In: *Philosophy and Public Affairs* 22.4 (1993), pp. 293–330.
- Ishani Maitra. "Silencing speech". In: *Canadian Journal of Philosophy* 39.2 (2009), pp. 309–338.

For readers who want to explore related topics in greater detail, I recommend:

- Alexander Bird. "Illocutionary silencing". In: *Pacific Philosophical Quarterly* 83 (2002), pp. 1–15.
- Anderson, Luvell and Michael Barnes, "Hate Speech", The Stanford Encyclopedia of Philosophy (Fall 2023 Edition), Edward N. Zalta & Uri Nodelman (eds.)
- Daniel Jacobson. "Freedom of speech acts? A response to Langton". In: *Philosophy and Public Affairs* 24.1 (1995), pp. 64–78.
- Jennifer Hornsby. "Disempowered speech". In: *Philosophical Topics* 23.2 (1995), pp. 127–147.
- Mary Kate McGowan. "Conversational exercitives and the force of pornography". In: *Philosophy & Public Affairs* 31.2 (2003), pp. 155–189.
- Rae Langton. "Beyond belief: pragmatics in hate speech and pornography". In: *Speech and Harm: Controversies over Free Speech*. Ed. by Ishani Maitra and Mary Kate McGowan. Oxford, UK: Oxford University Press, 2012.
- Saul, Jennifer, Esa Diaz-Leon, and Samia Hesni, "Feminist Philosophy of Language", The Stanford Encyclopedia of Philosophy (Fall 2022 Edition), Edward N. Zalta & Uri Nodelman (eds.)
- West, Caroline, "Pornography and Censorship", The Stanford Encyclopedia of Philosophy (Winter 2022 Edition), Edward N. Zalta & Uri Nodelman (eds.)

SLURS

Warning: This chapter is about slurs. Highly offensive expressions involving race, gender, sexual orientation, ability status, and similar will appear frequently in the discussion, and reference will sometimes be made to violence motivated by hate.

7.1 WHAT IS THERE TO SAY ABOUT SLURS?

In Chapter Six, we saw how philosophers have used the Austinian idea that speech involves action to throw light on questions of clear social and political significance. In this chapter, we will continue to follow that thread, although here in a way that ventures further into the gray zone mentioned at the end of Chapter Six, where Austin 'takes back' the sharp distinction between saying and doing and raises the possibility that most (or all) of our utterances involve elements of both.

Our focus here will be on slurs – expressions like the following:

> n★gger, j★gaboo, c★on, sp★c, w★tback, fa★got, h★mo, d★ke, tr★nny, cr★p, r★tard, limey, cracker, gringo …

The most obvious feature these expressions share, and the feature that philosophical theories of slurs are primarily concerned to explain, is

DOI: 10.4324/9781003250753-7

that they are *offensive*. Slurs can hurt or belittle people, make them angry or upset, and raise moral questions that many uses of language do not – except perhaps in certain special circumstances, someone who utters a slur seems to *do something wrong*.

This moral dimension is a key reason slurs have generated significant philosophical discussion – the topic seems pressing and socially relevant in a way that not every topic in the philosophy of language might. Despite this motivation, most of the philosophical literature on slurs is focused relatively narrowly on the linguistic side of things. The key question that shapes that literature, and the question that will guide our discussion here is: what *makes* these words offensive?

To sharpen that question a little, think about the slurs from the list above. Can you identify the social groups that each expression is typically used to target? I assume anyone who knows English well enough to be reading this book will know that the first word on our list is a slur whose paradigmatic uses pejorate Black people, that 'sp★c' targets people racialized as Hispanic, that 'f★ggot' is used against gay men, and so on.

While there is some debate among philosophers about whether slurs have **neutral counterparts** – that is, about whether there is always (or ever) a non-slurring expression that picks out exactly the same group as a slur would – it seems pretty clear that there's a sense in which at least *part* of the meaning of a slur involves a certain social group. Since it isn't obviously offensive to refer to groups of people in virtue of their race, gender identity, national origin, religion, sexual orientation, cognitive or physical ability status, etc., it seems like there must be something over and above this meaning that makes the slur offensive.

The kinds of philosophical questions about language that we have looked at so far in this book provide a set of possible ways we might go about saying what that something consists in. Speaking in very broad terms, I tend to see theories of slurs clustering into two families. On the one hand, there are theories that treat the offensiveness of slurs primarily in terms of the kinds of resources we looked at in Part One of the book, that is, in terms of some kind of *information* that people who use slurs put forward. On the other hand, there are theories that use the kinds of resources we have developed here in Part Two to do most of the explanatory work, that is, theories that focus on the *actions* slurs are used to realize. Of course, it's also possible to blend elements of these two approaches, and as our discussion progresses we will look at theories that do just that.

Where theories of the first sort are concerned, we find variation along all of the axes we looked at in Part One (and more). So, for example, we might offer a semantic treatment of slurs, saying that the offensive component is part of their truth-conditional meaning. Alternatively, we might try to involve the metasemantics – we could say, for example, that a slur and its neutral counterparts (or nearby expressions) don't fundamentally differ in meaning, but that the *way* in which the meaning of the slur is determined involves offensive elements. Or we could take a pragmatic route, claiming that the meaning of the slur is not inherently problematic, but that the kinds of messages sent when people use slurs are richer than their core meaning, and that the communicated contents *are* offensive.

We'll look at examples of several of these strategies below, and we'll see how a similar diversity of possibilities opens up if we think of slurring primarily in speech act terms. As has been the case throughout, our aim won't be to settle the question of what the best analysis of slurs is, so much as it will be to introduce you to the kinds of issues theorists who work in this area are grappling with and equip you with tools that will help you if you decide to read more on your own.

7.2 SHARPENING OUR FOCUS

Before we really get down to the task of looking at different treatments of slurs in detail, it will be worth walking through some other features philosophers take to be characteristic of them. Different philosophers have grouped them differently, and the lists you'll see in different places sometimes add a property here or drop one there, but there is broad agreement that in addition to the fundamental property of offensiveness, slurs differ from their alleged neutral counterparts with regard to the way in which they behave in a range of linguistic and social contexts that I'll present in this section. Having a sense of those contexts will allow us to better appreciate the forces that have shaped the various theories that have been proposed in the literature.

Variable offensiveness

The first point that I want to call attention to is that people's intu-itions about the offensiveness of slurs appear to come in degrees, as opposed to being on-or-off; this trait is often called **variable offensiveness**. The variable offensiveness of different slurs can be detected both if we compare slurs that pick out a single social group, as well as if we draw comparisons across groups. To see this, consider some different expressions that target the same groups. For exam-ple, I imagine that nearly everyone will agree that the n-word is somehow stronger or more offensive than 'c★on', which itself seems stronger than 'colored', which would nevertheless clearly not be an unmarked expression in contemporary usage. The same gradient can be detected between for example, 'f★ggot' and 'h★mo', and many other slurs.

Now consider expressions that target *different* groups. Even quite negatively charged expressions for white people that have a degree of common currency in English – like the Hawaiian expression 'haole' or the Latin American Spanish origin 'gringo' – seem pretty clearly to be less offensive than words that target people with minority social identities. Although we won't explore the reasons for this difference in any detail here – presumably it has to do with the comparative social power of the groups involved – it is worth call-ing attention to the fact that there is a difference. A good account of slurs should make room for explanations along these (or other) lines.

Many people have the intuition that a white person who uses the n-word does something more offensive than a Black person who uses it, even if we set aside so-called 'reclaimed' uses that plausibly involve building in-group solidarity. Again, while people who have this intu-ition will probably want to explain it in terms of facts that go beyond the philosophy of language, it might be a constraint on theories that they be compatible with plausible explanations here. (Alternatively, people who *do not* have this intuition might prefer theories that make it easy to explain why the social identity of the person who utters a slur does not change it offensiveness.)

Offensive autonomy

Another characteristic feature of the offensiveness of slurs involves something philosophers have sometimes called **offensive autonomy**. Offensive autonomy means that while the degree of offense associated with the utterance of a slur may vary in different circumstances, even the best intentions don't make the slur unoffensive. In other words, someone who says:

> I saw Kalle at the auto parts shop the other day. Having only worked with him over email, I hadn't realized he was a honky! We should invite him over sometime for a welcoming meal; we can serve some of that processed cheese spray they like, and maybe even some canned fruit and Cool Whip for dessert.

says something offensive, even if they're clearly trying to be friendly. (If 'honky' doesn't generate a clear enough intuition for you, replace it with another slur and try to imagine a parallel context involving 'friendly' intentions).

Entailment asymmetry

Another property that is often taken to be characteristic of slurs involves something called **entailment asymmetry**. Consider the following sentences, adapted from Hom (2007):

(30)   If Yao is a ch★nk, then he must be Chinese.

(31)   If Yao is Chinese, then he must be a ch★nk.

These sentences illustrate an asymmetrical relationship between what we can conclude on the basis of someone's being picked out by a slur, and their being picked out by a non-slurring expression for a group they belong to. Many people have had the intuition that even non-racists will in at least some vague and reluctant way accept a sense in which (30) sounds sort of true, while flatly and consistently denying (31). Along similar lines, Hom notes that people – racist or not – sometimes say things like:

(32)   Yao is Chinese, but he isn't a ch★nk.

A racist might use this sentence as a way of indicating that they consider Yao distinctive in a way that sets him apart from other Chinese people and makes him an inappropriate target of the slur. A non-racist might deny that Yao could be a ch★nk because they reject that way of thinking or talking about people completely.

Importantly, asymmetry in these two senses seems to be a general feature of slurs – variations on these templates appear to be constructible using all of the examples that we began this chapter with. While this piece of data leaves open quite a bit about the structure of slurs, it is nevertheless suggestive, and many philosophers have taken it to be another one of the things a good theory should explain.

Speaker orientation

Slurs are also different from neutral expressions where something called **speaker orientation** is concerned. Speaker orientation is the name given to the fact that someone who utters a slur does something offensive, even if their speech is meant not to represent their own beliefs but to report on the content of someone else's speech. Here are some examples from Renee Jorgensen, whose work we'll look more at below, that illustrate the phenomenon:

(33)   Bob said he'll fire all the c★nts.

(34)   Bob said he really likes that c★nt who recently took over the company.

Intuitively, someone who uses sentence (33) to address us does something offensive. This is true whether Bob himself used the word in question or not. If you produce sentence (33) in front of Grandma or the Queen, it is *you* who does something transgressive; Bob will not himself be implicated in the offense, even if he originally did use the slur. If you are in a context in which the precise words he used are relevant – like giving a deposition or testifying in Parliament – in order to defuse the offensiveness you have to go to comparatively extreme linguistic lengths, saying something like 'I'm sorry, but to report Bob's speech word-for-word, I'll have to use an expression I'd rather not use', or similar. Even then, if you actually produce the word in question, many listeners are likely to feel its force quite viscerally.

Sentence (34) makes a similar point but brings out a nuance. Ordinarily, embedding a clause under the locution 'so-and-so said that' allows the speaker to distance themselves from the contents and implications involved (this is why Donald Trump loves to say 'people are saying that…'). So, if I say 'Bob said he likes the person who recently took over the company', I'm not in any sense suggesting that *I* think highly of that person; my own attitudes aren't on display. But in the case of sentence (34), somehow my way of thinking bleeds through – in addition to causing offense, people who hear me say this will be left with the idea that I don't have a good view of the new boss.

Projection

The data that bring out the speaker orientation of slurs connect closely with a related feature that is relevant for many of the theories we will consider here: **projection**. To see what projection amounts to, consider the following sentences:

(35) Your friend is tall.

(36) Is your friend tall?

(37) If your friend were tall, I would want to know.

(38) It is not the case that your friend is tall.

The paradigm we've built with these four sentences may remind you of our discussion at the end of Chapter Five, where we distinguished between the force of a speech act and the content involved. In fact, the grammatical difference between the first sentence here and the second sentence does bring with it a difference in the kinds of speech acts the sentences can be used to realize – the first is an assertion, and the second a question involving the same content. The third and fourth sentences highlight a related, but importantly different point. If we take an ordinary declarative sentence like (35) and make it the antecedent of a conditional, as in (37), or embed it under a negation, as in (38), we end up with an assertion still, but not an assertion of the same content as the original. In other words, someone who utters (37) or (38) *does not* assert that the person they're addressing's friend is tall, even though that idea plays a role in the thing they do assert.

You might think of these environments as **content blockers** – although the content expressed by sentence (35) is in some sense a part of sentences (37) and (38), somehow that content doesn't end up being asserted by the person who utters one of those sentences. Contrast what happens when we replace our neutral predicate 'tall' with a slur:

(39)   Your friend is a cracker.

(40)   Is your friend a cracker?

(41)   If your friend were a cracker, I would want to know.

(42)   It is not the case that your friend is a cracker.

These sentences demonstrate that there is no attenuation of the degree of offensiveness associated with a slur when it is used in a question, the antecedent of a conditional, or under negation, compared to when it is used in a straightforward assertoric sentence. (Again, if the word 'cracker' doesn't elicit clear intuitions for you, try the test with a different slur.) Somehow the offensiveness of slurs gets past the content blocker – in the specialized language of the industry, offensiveness **projects out** of what are ordinary called 'entailment-cancelling' environments.

7.3   INFORMATION-BASED THEORIES

To summarize our discussion from the previous section, what we are looking for in a theory of slurs is a theory that can explain why slurs are offensive, and do so in a way that will allow us to make sense of the apparent data involving offensive variability, offensive autonomy, entailment asymmetry, speaker orientation, and projection. Here we will consider three information-type theories to see how well they meet those aims.

7.3.1   A TRUTH-CONDITIONAL ACCOUNT

The first theory we'll consider due to Christopher Hom. Hom says that what makes slurs offensive is a part of their core semantic content, that is, of the truth conditions they encode. He takes slurs to involve three distinct semantic elements: a non-racist description of a social group, a racist prescription for how members of that group should be treated, and a racist description of the group in terms that purport to justify the prescribed treatment.

The easiest way to see how this works is to consider an example. Hom thinks the slur 'ch★nk' means something like 'ought to be subject to higher college admissions standards, and ought to be subject to exclusion from advancement to managerial positions, and ... , because of being slanty-eyed, and devious, and good-at-laundering, and ... , all because of being Chinese' (Hom 2007, 431). So, someone who says 'Yao is a ch★nk' is literally saying that Yao ought to be subject to higher college admissions standards (etc.) because he is good at laundering (etc.) because he is Chinese'.

It is easy to see why slurs would be offensive if this theory were true. Nearly all of us would be shocked if someone were to say 'I believe that Chinese people ought to be subject to higher college admissions standards because their ancestry makes them devious'. It's offensive to select people for bad treatment on the basis of their ethnicity, and it's offensive to suggest that someone's ethnicity would *justify* such a treatment.

Hom's account also quite clearly provides us with the kind of tools we'd need to explain many of the other features of slurs that we sketched earlier. If slurs combine prescriptions about how to treat their targets with descriptive claims drawn from racist ideologies, then we can see how some slurs would be stronger than others in virtue of encoding different prescriptions and descriptions.

So, for example, if we understood the n-word as encoding the property of being such that someone ought to be subject to extrajudicial killing in virtue of being a criminal menace in virtue of enslaved African ancestry, that seems like a plausible explanation of why the expression is exceptionally offensive. By analyzing less offensive slurs using less drastic prescriptions or less extreme racist characterizations of group members, we can (arguably) generate less extremely offensive slurring expressions.

What about offensive autonomy? Hom's semantic theory seems like it could plausibly explain the fact that a well-intentioned speaker still does something offensive when they produce a slur, too. If 'ch★nk' means (in general paraphrase) 'should be treated badly for racist reasons', then whether you intend to endorse that prescription or not, by saying the word you at the very least give the impression that you intend to endorse it. That may be enough to explain intuitions about the offense caused, even if we should later find out you didn't really mean to say what you did. If you travel to a foreign country, for example, and make a hand gesture that you take to mean 'hello' but locals take to mean something offensive, you may still offend people even though you don't mean to. This feeling may very well persist even once they learn that you misunderstood the significance of your gesture.

Hom's theory – which we really out to think of as a recipe for constructing theories, by putting different things in the prescription and racist description slots associated with different expressions – also offers a clean explanation of the fact that sentences involving slurs seem to entail sentences involving their neutral counterparts, but not vice versa. If slurs are compounds formed from a neutral counterpart, together with some extra material, we would expect exactly that pattern. Entailment asymmetry, after all, is an ordinary feature of the relationship between sets and subsets. Compare:

(43)   If something is a red square, it is red.

(44)   If something is red, it is a red square.

If we accept Hom's theory, the entailment asymmetries slurs appear to produce can be treated as instances of the familiar part/whole relation; 'ch★nk' picks out a more specific property than 'Chinese' does, so it's not a surprise that someone could fail to meet that stricter criterion, while meeting the weaker one.

As we work our way through our list of features, it's been so far, so good for the semantic theory. When we come to data involving projection, however, the picture looks less rosy. When we looked at projection in our overview from the previous section, we saw how the contents of expressions used in certain environments – like in the antecedent of a conditional, or under negation – are typically 'blocked'. If the offensive component of a slur were part of its truth-conditional content, then, we should expect it to be blocked, too! But then what would explain the fact that slurs are still offensive when used in these environments? This is often taken to be a significant problem for semantic theories.

Speaker orientation also appears to be hard for the semantic theorist to explain. If I say, to adapt Jorgensen's example from earlier, 'Bob said that he thinks women should be paid less in virtue of their emotional oversensitivity in virtue of their hormonal profile but that he likes the woman who recently took over the company', there is no sense in which I myself as a reporter am committed to that offensive view. On the other hand, if I say 'Bob said he likes the c★nt who just took over the company', what I say is both extremely offensive and suggests that I am the person with the offensive view. But if 'c★nt' just meant the thing that is spelled out in the sentence above, as a semantic treatment would have it, what would explain this difference?

Hom has an answer to the challenges posed by projection and speaker orientation. Put simply, that answer is to say that our intuitions about offensiveness are not totally reliable and that we sometimes feel that something was offensive even when there aren't really good grounds for thinking it was. For example, he says, many people report feeling uncomfortable about the word 'niggardly'. But the meaning of that word is clearly unoffensive – it means 'miserly' or 'meager' – and it has no etymological relationship to the n-word at all.

> Do you think this is a satisfying answer? If we accept that some words are offensive – in the sense of causing feelings of offense – even when they have no offensive content, what reasons might we give for thinking that the offensiveness of slurs comes from their content?

Semantic treatments of slurs raise one other sort of question that I want to look at before moving on. Remember Kripke's arguments against the descriptivist theory of names that we looked at in Chapter Two? One of those arguments was based on the idea that if descriptivism were true, we would expect the truth of sentences like 'Aristotle taught Alexander' to be analytic – if 'Aristotle' means 'the teacher of Alexander', then it follows by logic alone that Aristotle taught Alexander.

Something similar seems like it would be the case if a semantic theory of slurs were true. If Hom is right, for example, that the offensiveness of the slur 'ch★nk' is due to the fact that it encodes a racist description of Chinese people and a prescription for racist treatment, we should expect sentences like 'If Yao is a ch★nk, then Yao should be subject to higher university admissions standards than other people' to be true as a matter of deduction. But many people have the intuition that no sentences like this *are* true, and not only because they reject the racist ideology involved. While the idea that there is some bad content encoded by slurs seems plausible in the abstract, when we actually go to put our finger on a specific property that all users of slurs are committed to, it's quite difficult to find an acceptable candidate. There might be stereotypes associated with certain slurs, like being lazy or prone to drinking or crime, that is, but these seem to be much less precise and uniformly agreed upon than we would expect if they were part of the content of the expressions involved.

7.3.2 A PRESUPPOSITIONAL ACCOUNT

We have just looked at a number of things that a semantic treatment of the offensiveness of slurs does well, and a number of things it does less well. As it turns out, one of the difficulties we raised for the semantic theory – the one involving projection – looks very similar to a challenge that linguists and philosophers have wrestled with for a long time in other contexts. That is the challenge of explaining a phenomenon called **presupposition projection**, and the similarities have led some philosophers to think that the offensiveness of slurs might in fact be a special case of that more general phenomenon.

An analogy with a point that came up in our discussion of Austin's speech act theory in Chapter Five will help to bring out what presuppositions are, and thus what presupposition projection amounts to. Remember Austin's thought that for a speech act to be performed, certain conditions typically have to be fulfilled? One of the kinds of conditions we looked at concerned the **background** against which the act is attempted. We illustrated that idea with the example of a magic spell, which can only be performed when the person who utters the words has certain objects in their pockets or is standing at the right place at the right time, or whatever.

Many linguists and philosophers have noticed that something like Austin's background condition seems to affect the kinds of things we can do when producing ordinary declarative sentences. As we've said many times over the course of this book, it's typical to think of the meaning of a sentence as its truth conditions, and to think that people who utter a sentence are aiming to say something true. One way in which someone could fail at this task would be to say something false – you might say 'it's raining' but be mistaken and end up saying something false. Another way in which you could fail would be to say something that is *neither true nor false*.

P.F. Strawson, a philosopher whose work serves as the foundation for much modern research on presupposition, provided a famous example of this kind of failure. Responding to Russell's claim (which we saw in Chapter Two) that sentences involving definite descriptions like 'the *F*' involve the assertion that there is a unique *F*, Strawson writes:

> [S]uppose someone were in fact to say to you with a perfectly serious air: 'The king of France is wise'. Would you say, 'That's untrue'? I think it's quite certain that you wouldn't. But suppose he went on to ask you whether you thought that what he had just said was true, or was false; whether you agreed or disagreed with what he had just said. I think you would be inclined, with some hesitation, to say that you didn't do either; that the question of whether his statement was true or false simply didn't arise, because there was no such person as the king of France.
> (Strawson 1950, 300)

This passage brings out the idea that some sentences can only be used to say things that are true or false when certain conditions are met – those conditions are the sentence's **presuppositions**. Strawson thought that definite descriptions, instead of involving an assertion to the effect that a certain thing exists, *presuppose* that it does. So, someone who utters a sentence involving the expression 'the king of France' only manages to say something with a determinate truth value if there is a king of France.

This discussion is related to our current project because presuppositions, like the offensiveness of slurs, project out of linguistic environments that typically block semantic contents. We can see this if we consider a sentence that introduces the presupposition that Danylo has a sister:

(45)   Danylo's sister is a mathematician.

Someone who utters (45) is clearly committed in a sense to Danylo's having a sister, even though they don't assert that he has one – what they say can only be true (or false) if he does. (To channel Strawson, think about what you'd say if someone said 45 to you, and you knew

Danylo didn't have a sister – it's be more natural to say 'you're under a misimpression' than it would to say 'that's false'.) The same commitment persists when the presupposition-introducing expression occurs in a question (which only makes sense if the presupposition is met), in the antecedent of a conditional, and under negation:

(46)   Is Danylo's sister a mathematician?

(47)   If Danylo's sister were a mathematician, she'd probably be better at math than him.

(48)   It is not the case that Danylo's sister is a mathematician.

Nothing we have said here explains *how* or *why* presuppositions project or where they come from in the first place. But the pattern in the two sets of data we have compared is instructive – the pattern we detected in offensiveness of slurs, that is, seems to be the same as the pattern brought out by these sentences involving the expression 'Danylo's sister'.

This has led some philosophers to say that what makes slurs offensive is not a feature of their truth-conditional content, but rather of the presuppositions they encode. As we saw to be true of Hom-style semantic theories, where we could generate a variety of specific proposals by mixing and matching different offensive components, so here can we build a wide variety of different presuppositional theories depending on exactly what things we take various slurs to presuppose.

Although I don't know of anyone who has endorsed a theory just like this, for illustration's sake, consider a presuppositional analogue of the example analysis Hom gave for 'ch★nk'. Imagine, that is, that the slur makes exactly the same truth-conditional contribution as a neutral counterpart that picks out Chinese people. In addition to that content, however, the slur encodes a racist pair of presuppositions – one corresponding to Hom's prescription for ill treatment and one to his descriptive justification.

Since it shares much of the structure of the semantic theory, a theory constructed along these lines can give essentially the same answers where questions about variable offensiveness and offensive autonomy are concerned – stronger and weaker slurs will be the result of more-or-less terrible racist prescriptions and descriptions' being presupposed, and slurs will seem offensive regardless of the speaker's intentions because people will assume that people who use them know what they presuppose.

Where entailment asymmetry is concerned, a broadly similar story can also be told. Here we can't say the difference in meaning between 'Chinese' and 'ch★nk' involves a whole-part relation, since the two expressions share a truth-conditional meaning. But there is a sense in which the upshot is the same. A presuppositional account of slurs would hold that whenever both a sentence involving a slur and a sentence involving its neutral counterpart have a truth value, they'll have the same value. But, as we saw in the case of our sentences involving the king of France, the different presuppositions associated with the slur mean that there will be some contexts in which it ends up with no truth value at all (when its presuppositions aren't met).

The major advantage a presuppositional theory would offer over a semantic theory, of course, concerns the projection data that were our leading focus of discussion in this subsection. But a presuppositional theory seems like it could plausibly improve on the semantic theory where the predictions involving speaker orientation are concerned, too. Even if I'm reporting someone else's speech, using the expression 'the king of France' seems to commit me to there being such a person, unless I take pains to draw air quotes around their words or add 'but I myself don't think there is any such king':

(49)   Olena said that the king of France is bald.

What about the considerations that we closed our discussion of the semantic theory with? There we said it seemed to be a demerit that semantic theories would make sentences like 'If Yao is a ch★nk, then he is good at laundry' logical truths. That consequence won't follow here, since nothing about laundry is part of the meaning of the slur.

Nevertheless, a form of our earlier worry persists. At its root, the heart of the entailment problem was that we didn't think that people who are familiar with the word 'ch★nk' will all agree on any particular racist description or prescription. That issue recurs if we try to import a Hom-style prescription/description structure into the presuppositions associated with slurring expressions. While all of the considerations we have looked at here make a presuppositional treatment look attractive from a structural perspective, things get trickier when it comes down to details and we have to say exactly what would be presupposed by any particular slur.

Because of this, people who defend presupposition accounts of slurs usually use quite 'thin' or 'bleached' presuppositions, like 'Jews deserve pejoration', 'Jews are despicable', or 'the speaker believes Jews deserve pejoration/are despicable/the speaker despises Jews'. As the presuppositions become less substantive, however, the extent to which we can rely on them to explain intuitions about variable offensiveness shrinks.

> Suppose you had to defend a presuppositional theory, on which what is presupposed is a thin – not robustly descriptive – negative attitude held by the speaker towards the group in question. How in this case might you explain intuitions about variable offensiveness? If the n-word and 'colored' both refer to the same group of people and both presuppose the speaker has a negative attitude, why should one be more offensive than the other?

7.3.3   PRAGMATIC ACCOUNTS

Another family of theories that has received a lot of attention from philosophers treats the offensiveness of slurs as a pragmatic phenomenon. You may recall from our discussion in Chapter Six that we struggled to draw a neat line showing where semantics ends and pragmatics begins; there we contented ourselves with a rough distinction between the linguistic meaning of a sentence and the thing that a speaker manages to use it to get across in a particular context. As an example, we said that while it's very clear that nothing about closing any windows or passing any sweaters is a part of the meaning of 'I am cold', speakers can easily use that sentence to get someone to close the window or pass them a sweater. Theorists who have endorsed pragmatic accounts of slurs claim that while their meanings – their truth-conditional contributions as well as their presuppositions – are the same as the meanings of any neutral counterparts, speakers who utter them somehow manage to communicate something offensive that goes beyond those meanings.

While there are many different varieties of pragmatic approach on offer in the literature, I want to look at a particular style of view that has become prominent in recent years. The kind of view I have in mind is based on the idea that in addition to knowing the meanings of words and knowing a set of principles for combining them, people who know a language have a lot of knowledge about what are called **linguistic metadata**.

A comparison with email systems or phone call logs can help us see what linguistic metadata are. Think of the information that you have access to when you read an email. On the one hand, you have the content of the mail itself – all of the propositions that are contained in the text. In addition to this, you have access to the information displayed in the header, concerning the time the email was sent, the address it was sent from, maybe the kind of device it was composed with, and so on. This latter sort of data is metadata – data about *how* the message was sent. The same kind of distinction can be drawn between the content of a conversation you have with a friend on the phone and the fact that you called a certain number at 18:22 on a certain date, from a certain number, speaking for a certain amount of time, and so on. While the content of your conversation won't make it into the kind of call logs that your mobile phone operator keeps, this sort of data *about* the call – metadata – is typically stored somewhere.

Now think about the kinds of things you know about the words in your vocabulary. Take 'behoove', for example, or 'beseech'. If you know what these words mean, and if the picture of language we developed here in Part One is on the right track, then you know how they contribute in a systematic way to the determination of the truth conditions of the sentences they occur in. But if you know these words, you probably *also* have a sense about how frequently they're used, maybe about how frequently they're used in relation to other words with similar meanings, what kind of contexts they're typically used in, and so on. You'll know that these are sort of old-fashioned words, more likely to occur in an academic or literary context than in contemporary popular fiction or casual conversation. This latter sort of knowledge is something you have in virtue of knowing something about the expressions' metadata and is the kind of thing recorded in dictionaries with labels like *archaic, vulgar*, and so on.

As far as I know, the first theory to employ linguistic metadata in an analysis of slurs was developed by Luvell Anderson and Ernest Lepore. Their theory, which they called **prohibitionism**, said essentially that slurs are offensive because people who utter them violate a prohibition that everyone in a language community knows about. In addition to knowing the meanings of slurs (this one applies to this group of people, that one to that other group), that is, Anderson and Lepore point out that ordinary speakers know that we aren't supposed to utter them! But doing things that you aren't supposed to do is a way of being impolite or aggressive. When they originally developed their theory, Anderson and Lepore claimed that this itself could be enough to explain why slurs seem offensive, and they supported their argument by pointing to cases in which the simple fact of someone's doing something prohibited causes offense.

In more recent work, a number of philosophers (including Anderson and Lepore themselves) have developed theories that employ more specific sorts of metadata to explain more precisely how offensiveness comes into the picture. The philosopher Renee Jorgensen and the linguist Geoffrey Nunberg, for example, have each developed versions of something Jorgensen calls the **contrastive choice** theory of slurs, which is well suited for this task. As the name suggests, the heart of this treatment is the idea that by choosing one expression over another that has the same meaning, we can send different pragmatic signals to our audience.

If we assume that the people we are talking to know, in addition to the meanings of the words we produce, a lot about what kinds of people typically use which words, what kinds of things they tend to believe, what contexts which words are typically used in, and so on, then we'll be able to reasonably expect that people will take our choice of one over another to be a way of sending a message.

For example, if your mother typically uses a short form of your name to address you when she is happy with you and a longer version when she is not, then when you hear the full version, you'll know that you are in trouble. If the two expressions in question didn't have the same meaning, you might think the reason for the choice was that she wanted to express a different truth condition – but if the meaning is the same, and the only difference is that one is used in friendly contexts and one in angry, you'll be able to guess that your mom wants you to know you're on thin ice!

Jorgensen and Nunberg apply this kind of thinking to the case of slurs by pointing out that in addition to knowing what groups they apply to, ordinary speakers of English know that they are words only racists use. In a pithy summary of the key point, Nunberg says:

> R*dskin* is distinguished from *Indian* not by any additional evaluative or expressive features of its meaning, but merely in being the description of Indians prescribed by the conventions of a group whose members have disparaging attitudes about American Indians. Then the implications of pointedly choosing to use *r*dskin* arise not from the meaning of the word but from its association with the discourse of a certain group of speakers... In a nutshell, racists don't use slurs because they're derogative; slurs are derogative because they're the words that racists use.
> (Nunberg 2018, 244, ★ added)

In our previous discussion, we saw how both Hom's semantic theory and the basic architecture of presuppositions could be used to generate a wide variety of different specific theories depending on what exactly we plug into which slots. A pragmatic theory based on the mechanism of contrastive choice has an even more open-ended structure. Jorgensen and Nunberg take it that what a person does in using a slur is signal to listeners that they hold racist attitudes, are members of a racist group, and similar. But part of the beauty of their theory is that they don't have to say exactly which attitudes are at stake – in fact, we wouldn't expect there to *be* any very specific attitude that is shared by everyone using a slur or even across the various occasions a particular person uses one. So, pragmatic theories offer a way of side-stepping the issue we raised for the other two theories about it not seeming to be true that there is any specific thing that is meant/presupposed by slurs.

Someone who endorses a theory like Jorgensen's or Nunberg's will also be able to easily explain why different slurs would be more or less offensive. Think of the different sorts of metadata that people know to be associated with an expression. On the one hand, we have information about who tends to use that word now, what kind of beliefs they tend to hold, what kinds of actions they tend to engage in. As the groups, beliefs, and actions become more and more extreme, the 'felt effects' produced by an invocation of the word will be more and more strong, too. The same goes for the *history* of the word – it seems plausible to think, as many philosophers have indeed held, that the particularly appalling history of anti-Black racism in the United States, with historical roots in slavery but encompassing violence long after, has a role to play in explaining the particular status of the n-word, for example.

Since theories of this sort locate the pragmatically relevant features of slurs in the metadata, as opposed to in their core content, someone who utters a slur at all – whether they are using it, or merely repeating it – activates those features. To see this, think about a case in which it's clear that I'm not trying to make an assertion, but am rather just producing some sounds to warm up my voice for singing. If I stand there and warm up by producing sounds that sound just like slurs, I will cause offense, in virtue of activating the associations those sounds have – why, you'll think, wouldn't I just use random sounds, if I hadn't meant to send a message? This means the metadata theorist has an explanation of the projection data, and of speaker orientation.

Where offensive autonomy is concerned, the pragmatic theory is in roughly the same situation as the semantic and presuppositional theories. Strictly speaking, the pragmatic theories we've looked at, like Grice's theory of implicatures, involve a speaker's intentions. The contrastive choice model turns on the assumption that the person is signaling by means of the contrast – if they didn't mean to signal, then we might say there really shouldn't be a pragmatic implication. But as we did in the previous two cases, we can explain this issue away to some extent by saying that most people will assume that someone who chooses the offensive member of a contrasting pair does so knowingly.

The contrastive choice theory does not provide nearly as obvious explanation of the data involving entailment asymmetry as the semantic and presuppositional theories did, but I'll leave it to you to decide how we should balance the pros and cons of each.

7.4 ACTION-BASED THEORIES

So far, the theories we have considered share a common feature: they take the fundamental kind of activity that people are involved in when they use slurs to be a signaling or message sending activity. The major differences between them concerned the kind of signal sent (a prescription about how certain people ought to be treated, perhaps together with a racist description of them, an attitude held by the speaker, etc.) and the way that signal is encoded (in the truth conditions, in the presuppositions, or pragmatically).

Knowing as you do about Austin's approach to language, however, you may have been thinking during our presentation about the ways in which we might explain offensiveness in more squarely *performative* terms. There are many ways a performance-focused account might be developed, and in fact, many ways in which such accounts have been developed. Here we will look at two that I think illustrate particularly philosophically important facets of the ways slurs are used and what those uses show about language more generally.

7.4.1 DISCOURSE ROLES AND POWER GRABS

The first account I want to take up is one proposed by Mihaela Popa-Wyatt and Jeremy Wyatt. Popa-Wyatt and Wyatt are clear that they think speakers who use slurs do a range of things at the same time, from signaling contempt to harming and degrading their targets. What they take to be at the real heart of the matter, however, and to fundamentally explain what's wrong with using slurs, recalls Langton and Hornsby's approach to pornography. There we saw how in addition to silencing women, pornography might be able to *subordinate* them, by laying down the 'rules of the game' in a way that puts women in a lower place in a hierarchy of power than men.

In order for the subordinating force of pornographic speech to count as subordinating, we saw that it was required that the pornographer be seen as authoritative in a certain sense. While there is obviously no legislative power granted to pornographers, Langton thought that pornographers have a degree of authority simply in virtue of the fact that consumers of pornography (in particular, men and boys) treat them as though they do. Popa-Wyatt and Wyatt have a similar take – they hold that simply by using a slur, a speaker can *seize* authority for themselves in an unjust way and subordinate those who are targeted by the slur.

The model Popa-Wyatt and Wyatt propose to explain this process depends on two key concepts: **social roles** and **discourse roles**. Social roles, they say, are constructs that 'carry information about permissible and expected behaviors, status, rights, and responsibilities' accorded to different people. Some last a lifetime, like ethnicity and gender, and some last for a short time, like being a customer in a restaurant.

Discourse roles are a special kind of particularly short-lived social role that we take on only for a specific conversation – they tell us who sets the questions that are up for debate, who talks in what order, who looks to whom for guidance, and so on. Discourse roles also help us make sense of the things people say. Remember our example involving words on a page that could constitute either a shopping list or a spy's report about what someone bought at the shop? In a variation, imagine a person who enters a bank and says 'I want a thousand dollars'. If we take the person to occupy the *customer* discourse role, we treat this utterance as a request. If we take the person to occupy the *robber* discourse role, we treat it as a demand.

Often, the discourse roles we play in a conversation are inherited from more stable social roles that we occupy in the background; if I see you're wearing a police uniform, that'll structure my verbal interaction with you. But we can also use the way we speak to *establish* ourselves in the discourse roles we want and to try and *assign* discourse roles to others.

Imagine a visitor who comes into your office, puts their feet up on your desk, and lights a cigarette. You might think that in addition to sending you the message 'I'm in charge here', there's a sense in which their action actually *makes* it the case that they are – the proof is right there in the smoke cloud! As I understand Popa-Wyatt and Wyatt, their view is that someone who uses a slur does something like this. Everyone knows that slurs are associated with a long and brutal history that involves clear patterns of dominance. If I target you with a slur, I put myself in a position of power, and in so doing, put you in a comparatively less powerful position.

Popa-Wyatt and Wyatt think the difference in the degree of offense associated with different uses of slurs comes down to the degree of injustice associated with this kind of power grab. Slurs that have a particularly long or repulsive history will involve larger seizures of power than expressions with less historical weight behind them. The theory is also well-positioned to explain projection, speaker orientation, and offensive autonomy. Like the pragmatic theories based on linguistic metadata, Popa-Wyatt and Wyatt can say that simply uttering a slur is a power grab, whether it's in the antecedent of a conditional or in someone else's reported speech, and regardless of what your intention was in uttering it.

The discourse role theory is like the contrastive choice theory in not making entailment asymmetry a central explanatory aim. Again, it'll be up to you to decide how much of an issue this is!

7.4.2 SIGNALING IN ACTION

The last analysis of slurs that we will look at here is a kind of hybrid theory, combining elements of the signaling theories we looked at in the previous section with elements of the kind of more performatively oriented approach sketched immediately above. The theory, developed by Elisabeth Camp, holds that 'slurs are so rhetorically powerful because they signal allegiance to a perspective: an integrated, intuitive way of cognizing members of the targeted group' (2013, 335).

On the face of things, this might seem reminiscent of Hom's semantic theory – Hom, recall, held that slurs encode a description of a target group that derives from a racist ideology, together with prescriptions about how members of the group should be treated in virtue of their having the properties the description alleges. That sounds not too far from 'an integrated, intuitive way of cognizing members of the target group'. In contrast to Hom's view, which is that people who use slurs are literally asserting that members of the group ought to be treated a certain way, Camp seems to be saying something slightly weaker. I might, after all, 'signal allegiance' to the view that certain people ought to be treated a certain way without actually asserting as much – by flying certain flags, say, or dressing a certain way.

So is Camp presenting a variation on the semantic theory? She takes the extension of a slur – the set of individuals it picks out – to be the same as the extension of a neutral counterpart. We might wonder, then, if the core commitment of her theory is to there being another level of semantic content, something like a Fregean sense, a mode of presentation of a certain referent. Whether the Fregean analogy holds up or not, if we look a bit more closely at Camp's notion of perspective, we can appreciate some quite important differences between her view and classical 'signaling' views.

Building on the 'intuitive' part of her initial description, Camp says:

> On my understanding, perspectives are modes of interpretation: open-ended ways of thinking, feeling, and more generally engaging with the world and certain parts thereof (Camp 2006, 2008, 2009). Above all, perspectives are ongoing dispositions to structure one's thoughts, along at least two dimensions. First, a perspective involves dispositions to notice and remember certain types of features rather than others, so that those features are more prominent or salient in one's intuitive thinking, and have more influence in determining one's classifications (cf. Tversky 1977). Second, a perspective involves dispositions to treat some classes of features as more central than others, in the sense of taking those features to cause, motivate, or otherwise explain many others.
> (Camp 2013, 336)

While it might be possible to frame some of what makes a certain perspective the perspective it is in propositional terms – by saying things like 'Chinese people ought to be treated poorly in virtue of being good at laundry' or whatever – the really interesting things that happen in this passage involve 'dispositions to notice and remember certain types of features rather than others' and 'taking those features to cause, motivate, or otherwise explain' others.

Consider an example Camp herself often employs when presenting her work on perspectives:

Figure 7.1: Drawing by Stephen Laurence, used with permission

What do you see when you look at this picture? Can you see anything else? If not, keep looking. Once you are able to see each of
the two images, think about what has changed. All of the ink on the
page is in the same place. The light in the room is the same, as is the
distance and the angle between your eye and the page. To 'flip' the
valence of the image that you're seeing – to go from seeing an old
woman to a young one – what changes is which features are salient
to you, and how you take them to fit together.

Camp's notion of the kind of perspective that is at issue where
slurs are concerned is a notion that reproduces many of these features. While a perspective may encompass negative beliefs about a
target group, it doesn't have to. We can imagine a perspective that
doesn't involve any particular beliefs at all, but which rather shapes
the way in which we attend to members of the group – what kind
of things we focus on, what kind of things stand out. Where the
perspectives associated with slurs are involved, Camp thinks, the perspectives involved will be negative ones, ones that play a role in our

cognitive dynamics that redounds to the disadvantage of the people targeted, that is, which makes us think worse of individuals from the group, or the group itself.

The fact that different perspectives will be associated with different slurs gives Camp the resources to explain why some slurs are more offensive than others. The really remarkable thing about her view, though, and the thing that makes it much more than just another 'signaling' theory, is the way it approaches projection, speaker-orientation, ineffability, and the like.

Consider the old woman/young woman picture again. Try and put yourself in a frame of mind where you can't see both images or pretend you're addressing a friend who'd never seen them before, and only sees one of the two. Think about what you might do in order to get the person to see the other – you can say things like 'try and see the choker as a mouth, and the jawline as a nostril'. By saying things like this, you can get the person you're talking with to experience a 'flip', a kind of involuntary reorganization of the visual field. Your words can cause it to be the case that what looked like a young woman transforms into an old one. Interestingly, this effect is one that it can be quite difficult for listeners to resist. If they hear you and understand what you're saying, whether they want to see the old woman or not, she appears. It's a bit like an old saw from George Lakoff – if someone says 'whatever you do, don't think of an elephant!', there's a sense in which they have trapped you – you can't not think of the elephant!

If Camp is right that slurs encode perspectives and that people who use them signal allegiance to those perspectives, there is a sense in which the perspective associated with a slur ends up being forced on anyone who hears it. Whether you agree or disagree with whatever the perspective proscribes, reflectively endorse it or not, simply in virtue of processing the utterance you come into contact with the perspective in a way that has at least the potential to organize your thinking in the way someone does when they say 'don't think of the elephant' or 'see, her chin is her nose'.

As Camp puts things, when we come into contact with slurs:

> The speaker seems to have foisted on us, not just a claim, which we can deny, but something more amorphous, which escapes direct challenge. As a result, it seems that any standard form of engagement with the slurring utterance threatens to make us complicit in the bigot's way of thinking, despite our finding it abhorrent.
> (Camp 2013, 330)

Camp's view is that slurs provide a particularly striking illustration of a feature of language that is in fact totally general; her notion of perspective and the way we can affect one another by deploying words that encode perspectives puts a new shine on Austin's thought that all speech has performative and constative elements.

FURTHER READING

Key sources for the material presented in this chapter include:

- Luvell Anderson and Ernest Lepore. "What did you call me? Slurs as prohibited words". In: *Analytic Philosophy* 54.3 (2013), pp. 350–363.
- Renee Bolinger. "The pragmatics of slurs". In: *Noûs* 51.3 (2017), pp. 439–462.
- Elizabeth Camp. "Slurring perspectives". In: *Analytic Philosophy* 54.3 (2013), pp. 330–349.
- Christopher Hom. "The semantics of racial epithets". In: *Journal of Philosophy* 105.8 (2008), pp. 416–440.
- Geoffrey Nunberg. "The social life of slurs". In: *New Work on Speech Acts*. Ed. by Daniel Fogal, Daniel Harris, and Matt Moss. Oxford University Press, 2018, pp. 239–291.
- Mihaela Popa-Wyatt and Jeremy L. Wyatt. "Slurs, roles, and power". In: *Philosophical Studies* 175 (2018), pp. 2879–2906.

For readers who want to explore related topics in greater detail, I recommend:

- Anderson, Luvell and Michael Barnes, "Hate Speech", The Stanford Encyclopedia of Philosophy (Fall 2023 Edition), Edward N. Zalta & Uri Nodelman (eds.)

- Bianca Cepollaro. "In defense of a presuppositional account of slurs". In: *Language Sciences* 52 (2015), pp. 36–45.
- Claudia Bianchi. "Slurs and appropriation: an echoic account". In: *Journal of Pragmatics* 66 (2014), pp. 35–44.
- Justina Díaz-Legaspe, Robert Stainton, and Chang Liu. "Slurs and register: a case study in meaning pluralism". In: *Mind and Language* 35.2 (2020), pp. 156–182.
- Luvell Anderson and Ernest Lepore. "Slurring words". In: *Noûs* 47.1 (2013), pp. 25–48.
- Robin Jeshion. "Pride and prejudiced: on the appropriation of slurs". In: *Non-Derogatory Uses of Slurs*. Ed. by Cepollaro and Zeman. Grazer Philosophische Studien, 2018.

LINGUISTIC DIVERSITY

Warning: The n-word appears several times in this chapter on page 178, in a passage quoted from Langston Hughes.

8.1 OVERVIEW

So far, this book has been structured around indisputably core topics in the philosophy of language. If you'd taken a course in the subject at a major university in the English-speaking world anytime since 1980 or so, you'd almost certainly have covered all of the material from Part One. While much of the material from Part Two is more recent, I think it is fair to say that it has achieved a similarly canonical status and I imagine that to someone looking back from 2050 or so, the social and political philosophy of language will be as clearly an indispensable part of an introductory syllabus as the material from Part One is (in many places, this is already true).

For this final chapter, I want to do something a bit different. Instead of presenting more material from another established literature, I want to engage in a freer exploration of what I myself happen to think are some interesting questions that can be usefully addressed using the tools we have developed in the book. (If you like, you can think of this chapter as a kind of capstone demonstration of the kind

DOI: 10.4324/9781003250753-8

of thing we can do by weaving all of the different threads established in the book so far together. There are, of course, many other ways such a demonstration might go – if the book can play a small role in helping you to think about some of those, it will have been a success!) Put broadly, the topic I want to explore here is linguistic diversity. I assume that linguistic diversity is a good thing, and the question I will structure my discussion around is the question of what *makes* it good.[1]

Before getting started, let me register a few observations about the kind of answer I'll give. In general, questions like 'what is good about *x*?' are questions that admit of more than one response. To take a point of comparison that sounds silly but makes the point, think about tacos. What is good about them? For one thing, they're delicious. But they're also comparatively inexpensive. They can be eaten with your hands, which means you don't need silverware (or have to wash it afterwards). Everyone can add just the fillings they like, so there aren't fights about what to order.

In short, tacos have many virtues, and it does not seem like it would be very illuminating to get bogged down in an argument about which of those virtues is greater than the rest. I think linguistic diversity is a bit like tacos in this regard. Many things make linguistic diversity valuable, and my aim here will be to show how the philosophy of language can help us to appreciate some of those things, rather than to argue that one is more important than or serves as the foundation for the others.

Finally, let me note at the beginning that we might raise questions about linguistic diversity in two senses. On the one hand, we can talk usefully about diversity as measured across languages. So, a world in which people speak Swedish, Sami, and English is a world that is more linguistically diverse than a world in which people only speak English. On the other hand, we can also talk sensibly about diversity *within* a language – that is, the kind of diversity that's at stake when we distinguish Singapore English from Multicultural London English, or Ume Sami from Southern Sami. I hope to say enough about diversity in each of these senses here to get you started thinking about the issues that come up, but I'll leave it to you to decide how similar or different you think the cases are, and indeed, to decide whether you think the considerations I sketch here hold up.

8.2 WHAT IS LOST WHEN A LANGUAGE DISAPPEARS?

One of the ways to appreciate the value of something is to think about what would be lost if it were to disappear. Unfortunately, in the case of languages, we do not have to resort to any very exotic thought experiments in order to do this. While no one knows for sure, linguists estimate that there are somewhere in the vicinity of 7000 languages spoken on Earth today. By the end of the century, however, it is expected that about half of these will be gone.

Many people share the intuition that with each language that disappears, something valuable is lost. Prominent publications like *The New York Times* and *The Guardian* feature stories about dying languages depressingly frequently. My guess is that some of the interest these stories generate is due to the poignancy of the personal situation the last speakers of a language find themselves in – imagine there being just a few people in the world you could converse with in the language of your childhood! I suspect that the reason these stories resonate so widely, though, is that they are more than stories of individual loss – they are stories that point toward a kind of diminishment that affects us all, even if it is not one we would otherwise have been aware of.

The phenomenon of language extinction seems pretty clearly to involve substantial philosophical questions. From the perspective of ethics and political philosophy, for example, we might wonder about the kinds of social and political structures that lead to it and about what we could or should do to protect languages from extinction in the first place. From the perspective of metaphysics, we might wonder about whether it's possible to recover extinct languages – what would have to be the case to make the resurrected version a version of the same language that disappeared? Somewhat oddly, however, from the perspective of the philosophy of language it can appear less clear that there is really much significant at stake.

When people address the question of what is lost with a language in the popular press, the answers that come up most often are answers that don't seem to have a lot to do with language, per se. So, for example, we sometimes hear people say that if we allow languages to go extinct, we risk losing access to traditional knowledge about plant species or fungi that could be useful in developing things like new medical treatments. Those would certainly be forms of knowledge that it would be bad to risk or to actually lose, but the connection between the value of the knowledge in question and of the language spoken by the people who have it isn't obvious. If what we really cared about was plants or fungi or their utility, it seems like it would be easy enough to send scientists out to learn about them from the relevant experts, without necessarily learning anything substantial about the language those experts speak.

Occasionally, people offer an argument related to the one I've just sketched, but which aims for a stronger conclusion. Instead of claiming that people who know a certain language might possess some knowledge about the world that people who don't know that language lack, the argument I have in mind holds that there are things that you literally *couldn't* know, or at least, couldn't *express*, if you didn't have access to a certain language.

The most famous example of an argument like this involves the idea that people who speak certain Arctic languages have far more words for snow than people who don't speak those languages. So, what in English we would pick out using the word 'snow' would allegedly be picked out in one of these languages by 11 different non-overlapping words, or 15, or 19. Because of this difference, the argument goes, people who speak English fail to be able to draw distinctions when talking – or thinking! – about snow that people speaking languages with a more fine-grained vocabulary can draw.

If this argument were good, it seems like it would offer at least one straightforward way for us to respond to the question about what we lose when languages disappear – we'd lose the ability to say certain things and maybe even to think them in the first place! That seems like it'd be a pretty substantial loss.

Unfortunately for those of us who are interested in questions about the value of linguistic diversity, however, few linguists or philosophers think this snow argument is a good one. For one thing, it doesn't actually seem to be right that English is limited in its snow vocabulary in the way the argument supposes – people who care about snow and snow structures distinguish 'champagne powder' from 'Sierra cement', 'boilerplate' from 'dust on crust', and 'soft slabs' from 'hard slabs', to mention but a few examples used by laypeople.

Avalanche forecasters and snow scientists employ specialized language distinguishing forms of snow in much more fine grain than this.

Even if it did turn out to be the case that some languages had fewer words for snow than others do, though, that doesn't seem like it would amount to a very substantial limitation on the kinds of things people speaking those languages could say to one another. Recall our discussion from Chapter One about productivity and compositionality – there we pointed out how the challenge of constructing a theory of meaning is the challenge of constructing a theory that will allow you to say an unboundedly large number of things. In fact, most linguists and philosophers think that languages are equivalent in terms of the meanings they can be used to express. Someone speaking a language that lacks the snow word 'graupel' can always say 'soft, opaque pellets from 2 to 5mm in diameter', and if they find themself saying that often enough, they can introduce a shorter name for the stuff.

Finally, but perhaps for us most importantly, empirical research simply doesn't provide much support for the hypothesis of **linguistic determinism**, or the idea that the language you speak has very dramatic effects on your ability to do things like distinguish different sorts of snow in perception or cognition. So, even if the languages you speak don't have any expression like 'graupel', if you encounter the stuff in the world, you'll be able to see that it's different from other forms of snow. If it matters to you, you'll be able to remember it, see how to interact with it, and so on. (While it's important to recognize that anecdotes are not a substitute for empirical research, as a Californian living in the Arctic, I can confirm that neither my past experiences nor my identity as an English-speaker prevent me from making very fine-grained distinctions between dozens of kinds of frozen precipitation.)

If it doesn't turn out to be true, though, that there are thoughts that can only be had by speakers of a certain language, or things that can only be said in a certain language, is there any reason for the philosopher of language to care about linguistic diversity? In the next two sections, I'll try to provide a positive answer to this question by looking at differences in the range of things we can *do* when speaking a different language or dialect.

8.3 LANGUAGE-SPECIFIC ACTIONS

In this section, I will focus on the question 'What do we lose when languages disappear?', before turning my attention in the next section to a parallel question about dialectical diversity. Drawing on our discussion from Chapter Five and Chapter Six, the answers I'll give in both cases involve the *kinds* of things we can *do* in speaking – that is, the illocutionary actions we can undertake.

At the end of Chapter Five, we saw how we might construct a taxonomy for different types of illocutionary acts by distinguishing a variety of features, like the contents they involve, their illocutionary force, their direction of fit, and so on. Consider, for example, the following sentences:

(50)   The door is shut.

(51)   Shut the door.

(52)   Is the door shut?

At the level of description at which philosophers would typically characterize illocutionary actions, the actions someone could perform by uttering one of these sentences are distinguished in terms of their illocutionary force. Although they share a content – something involving a certain door – the first sentence is used to make an assertion, the second to give an imperative, and the third to pose a question.

Although this isn't traditionally part of what we study when we do speech act theory, anyone old enough and linguistically sophisticated enough to be reading this book will recognize that within each of these broad classes of speech act, we can also distinguish a range of different subtypes. So, in addition to assertions, demands, questions, and so on, we recognize that there is such thing as a class of polite or impolite questions, more and less forceful imperatives, and assertions that involve different degrees of conviction (to mention just a few sources of variation).

Sometimes what distinguishes illocutionary actions along these dimensions is the background they're set against – what it's polite to talk about or ask about may vary depending on who you are speaking with and how close your relationship is. While that seems like more of a social question than a linguistic one, there are also standard ways of marking the sentences we utter that predictably change their status. You can use the tone of your voice, for example, to make a request more or less strong, and in some languages different morphological or syntactic structures would let you do that, too.

I take this to reveal that there are at least two levels of description at which ordinary language users keep track of what kinds of illocutionary actions are being realized when people speak. Suppose you're watching a TV show together with a friend, in a language that you speak but they don't. If you're giving a play-by-play account of the action on the screen, sometimes it will be enough to say 'Participant *A* asked Participant *B* if they wanted to go on a date'. If your friend asks why Participant *A* is smiling, for example, it might be enough of an answer to say that they asked *B* on a date and *B* said yes.

There are other times, though, where explaining what has happened requires more detail – if your friend asks why you laughed at a certain scene, you might have to be more precise and say 'Participant *A* asked Participant *B* if they wanted to go on a date, but they did it in a cheeky way'. For some purposes, that is, a level of resolution at which we chop up the class of speech acts only into broad categories like assertions, questions, and imperatives won't be quite enough. To properly explain an interaction that's taking place, we sometimes have to zoom in, looking inside each of those categories to distinguish cheeky questions from demure ones, or whatever.

While some philosophers that I think highly of would resist this move, I myself think that ordinary speakers track the illocutionary actions that are performed around them (and which they themselves might perform) in even more fine grain than this. So in addition to distinguishing questions from assertions and polite questions from cheeky ones, I think we recognize types of actions whose identity depends on the *particular words* and grammatical structures that are used to perform them. Sometimes, if we want to provide a good explanation of what has happened in a conversation, or explain why someone reacted the way they did to something someone else said, we have to invoke this even more detailed level of description.

What is this even more detailed level, and how do we put it to work? Remember that in Chapter Seven, we looked at a cluster of analyses of slurs that involved linguistic metadata. The key to those analyses was the idea that in addition to knowing what words mean, typical speakers of a language know a lot about the contexts in which they tend to be used, and by whom. We know, for example, that certain words are usually produced by younger people, and certain others by older people. We know that certain words tend to be used by people who spent a long time in formal education, and others by people who spent less. We know how words are related to one another in virtue of sounding similar, or looking similar when written on the page, and we know about which words cluster with one another stylistically. For some words, we know things about their histories, or about particularly prominent occasions on which they were used.

All of these facts – together with the fact that we know that everyone knows them – contribute to shaping the set of illocutionary possibilities that are available to us. What you can do by using a word, that is, depends on what the word means, but also on how it sounds, what associations it activates with groups of people, ideologies, or other words, and what kind of historical background it has. But this raises the possibility that there will be speech acts that you can perform while speaking one language that you cannot perform while speaking any other language.

Unfortunately, the clearest way I know of illustrating this point is to consider a particularly upsetting example involving the n-word. In developing the theory of slurs we considered in Chapter Seven, Geoffrey Nunberg quotes a passage from Langston Hughes' autobiography *The Big Sea*. I follow Nunberg in reproducing the passage in its entirety, as it seems that is the best way to do justice to the point Hughes makes:

> The word *nigger* sums up for us who are colored all the bitter years of insult and struggle in America: the slave-beatings of yesterday, the lynchings of today, the Jim Crow cars, the only movie show in town with its sign up FOR WHITES ONLY, the restaurants where you may not eat, the jobs you may not have, the unions you cannot join. The word *nigger* in the mouths of little white boys at school, the word *nigger* in the mouth of the foreman at the job, the word *nigger* across the whole face of America!

As I read this passage, and as I understand Nunberg's invocation of it, Hughes offers a philosophically sophisticated take on what exactly is done when someone uses the n–word. Hughes thinks that such a person does more than just signal that they have a certain belief system or express racial animosity. As Nunberg puts things, they 'materially obtrude' the whole history of the expression into the present context – 'all the bitter years of insult and struggle in America'. This is why the slur has the force it does – it is a punch with the weight of that history behind it.

Slurring is a kind of illocutionary action that is possible in every language I know, and unfortunately, I suspect, likely possible in every language. The languages I know of all involve slurs that intuitively come in more and less weak forms; so in addition to the broad action type 'slurring' it seems plausible to think that more fine-grained types like 'extremely offensive slurring' and 'somewhat less extremely offensive slurring' are types of actions that can be performed in different languages. I think the example of the n–word, however, makes clear that there is a *certain very precise kind* of slurring action that you can only perform while speaking English. To do exactly the thing that someone does in uttering the n–word – to 'materially obtrude' the history of that word into the present context in the way you do when you produce that word – you have to actually produce that word.

To be clear, I do not mean to suggest that this is a *good* thing to be able to do or that this illocutionary action type is a type that we would have reason to mourn if it were to disappear from our inventory of options. I use this example because I think it is an especially powerful illustration of a point that applies totally generally: what we can do with our words sometimes depends on very specific properties they have, which are not properties shared by other expressions from the same language, much less by expressions from other languages.

Making a complete list of all of the kinds of properties that might be implicated in this kind of specificity would require a book of its own. But let me give an example of one other sort that I think is illustrative. We've just seen how the things you can do with a word depend at least in part on its history. Now I want to point out how the location a word occupies in a network of associations – even quite superficial associations, like what other words it sounds like – can matter where its illocutionary potential is concerned. I follow Ernest Lepore and Matthew Stone in using the following passage from Andrew O'Hehir, writing for the online version of Salon magazine:

> Should we stop using the adjective 'niggardly,' because it accidentally resembles another word?
>
> ... Along with roughly 100 percent of the media, I thought that controversy was ludicrous when it came up in the late '90s and early 2000s: If we consult the dictionary, we learn that 'niggardly' can be traced back to Middle English and Old Norse, and has no etymological connection to the racial slur. But I have to say that my perspective has since shifted. We pretty much have dumped that word, because it is so easily misunderstood and other words will do, and also because it carries a permanent taint: The only person who would conceivably use it now would be a snickering, anti-p.c. asshole trying to make an obnoxious point.
> (O'Hehir 2015)

I think O'Hehir's observation about what can be done in English nowadays is exactly right. At least in North America or the United Kingdom, if you insist on describing someone's behavior as 'niggardly' instead of 'stingy' or 'miserly', in almost any context that I can imagine you will come off as a quite specific type of pedantic jerk. Why is that? Well, for one thing, as O'Hehir mentions, because we have the words 'stingy' or 'miserly' in our vocabulary. This means that if you want to express the meaning those three words share, you can do so without using a word that happens to sound very much like the most highly proscribed slur in our language. If you do choose to use 'niggardly' – knowing about the equivalents and knowing that everyone else does – normal listeners will take your choice to have been intentional, and it's hard to imagine reasons for it that don't involve your posturing as some kind of provocateur.

The fact that 'niggardly' is both an antiquated and a low-frequency word – while I'm no corpus linguist, Google n-gram indicates its uses have been in steady decline from a peak around 1850 – plays a role in contributing to this sense. Although the facts about contrastive choice – why pick 'niggardly' when you could have picked 'stingy'? – would stand on their own, if we consider an alternative history of English in which the word 'niggardly' had always been more common than 'stingy', the effect might not have been so strong. In English as it has in fact developed, though, someone who chooses to say 'niggardly' not only does so in the face of clear alternatives that don't remind anyone of the n-word but reaches deep into the mists of time to do so.

I take our discussion of these two examples to show that the particular type of speech act that can be performed using a certain word depends on a range of highly particular facts about the word. The case of the n-word shows that a word's history matters – often giving a satisfying answer to questions like 'why was that offensive?' or 'why was that poignant?' or 'why did that make you laugh?' will require you to invoke the backstory associated with the words used. The case of 'niggardly' shows that the particular place a word occupies in the network of other words we have access to matters, too – that network is defined in terms of the meanings of words, their sounds and shapes, their relative frequencies, and so on.

But if we have shown that the particular type of speech act that can be performed using a certain word depends on highly particular facts about the word, then we have indeed identified a sense in which different languages will make different classes of speech acts possible. Every word in every language has its own history, which it shares with no other word. Furthermore, the structure of the network formed by those words and their associations is not a structure that will be repeated in any other language. In short: to do exactly the kind of action someone does when they hurl the n-word at someone, or the kind of action done by employing 'niggardly' instead of 'miserly', you have to be speaking English and using those words.

Now, so far, nothing we have said does much to help identify any source of *value* associated with this pair of action types. In fact, it seems pretty clear that if the two kinds of action we've focused on were to be lost somehow, we would not lose anything worth lamenting. Remember, though, that our two examples are meant to serve as particularly clear illustrations of a point that applies perfectly generally.

As I see things, nearly every time we address someone, we are maneuvering our way through a massive space of possible speech acts, individuated in extremely fine grain. Even once we have decided that the thing to do is to tell someone it's raining, that is, or ask them to close the window, we have a huge range of choices about *how* to do that. Those choices involve words that have different histories, associations with different groups of speakers and other words, and much more.

Although there isn't room here to give a fully developed argument in support of this claim, I take the choices we make about which of these very precise speech acts to perform to be choices that literally constitute us as the kinds of people we are, socially speaking. Think about the you that your friends and family are acquainted with – the character that they know. Are you a playful person? Serious? Charming? Now think about what your playfulness consists in, or your seriousness, or your charm. To some extent, certainly, actions that you take that have nothing to do with language play a role here – you could establish a playful identity without ever speaking by arranging slapstick pranks or making funny faces at children (say).

On the other hand, I think it is hard to avoid the fact that there is a large extent to which the kinds of actions that make you playful *are* actions you take in speaking. Imagine someone who never does anything like arranging a prank or making funny faces at children. Such a person could still very well count as playful in virtue of doing playful things with their speech, like making puns, rhyming, or deploying devices like double entendre.

Now, I think there is no question that people can be playful while speaking different languages. They can also be playful in the somewhat more specific way of making puns, rhyming, or deploying double entendre. But if we take a particular playful person and look at all of the playful speech episodes they have been involved in over the course of their life, I think we can appreciate a sense in which the particular *way* their playfulness manifests depends on the language(s) they speak. Could someone be playful in just the way dear Uncle Jimmy is playful without speaking the language he speaks – without that accent and that half-laughing intonation, without his characteristic malapropisms?

I don't think so. On my view, the way your playfulness (seriousness, poetic sensibility, etc.) manifests itself *is a part of* the you your friends know and love. I don't mean this as a metaphor – I think your social self is something you perform, something that is woven together out of all of the different actions you take over the course of your life. Many of those actions are speech acts, which each have one or another fine-grained character determined by all of the sorts of features we have referred to here.

When we lose a language, then, I think we lose a set of possible performances, which means a set of ways of constituting a self. If you know more than one language, think of the way you come across when speaking one or another or the way you experience the personalities of your friends and family when they address you in one or the other language – people seem different in different languages, right? While your fundamental personality traits would presumably survive if you somehow lost access to one of your languages after a bump on the head, I think there is a very real sense in which a 'you' would be gone. By the same token, while traits like seriousness or playfulness do not depend on any particular language, the very set of ways a person might construct a self by being playful in Achuar disappears if Achuar does.

While I think a world in which there are fewer ways of bringing a self to life by performing is a world that is in an important sense less rich for all of us, this way of thinking about things also helps to make sense of what is so poignant about the situation the last speakers of a language find themselves in. If it's right that self-creation is something we do by performing speech acts, and if Austin is right about the idea that a speech act only counts as being performed when the uptake condition is met, then it follows that if you are speaking a language no one else understands, you are not able to perform the actions in it that you would be able to if you had an audience that understood. In some of my work, I've compared this situation to a gifted musician playing sophisticated and beautiful music that no one can hear. In fact, the analogy is only partially apt – if Austin is right, there is a sense in which the music isn't really being played at all.

8.4 DIALECTICAL DIVERSITY

If the argument I sketched in the previous section is on the right track, different languages provide their speakers with different materials to use in constructing a social identity. To lose a language, then, is to lose a set of possible identities. In this section, I want to briefly explore some consequences of the fact that something similar seems to be true of the resources provided by different dialects, or ways of speaking a particular language.

So far, whenever we've talked about meaning over the course of this book, we've had something quite specific in mind. Early in Chapter One, we looked at reasons for thinking that what it is to know the meaning of a sentence is to know what truth condition it expresses, and in the rest of Part One we looked at a variety of philosophical questions that conception of meaning leaves open. Up until this point in Part Two, the notion of meaning has played a less explicit role in our discussion. Instead of asking 'what does this sentence mean?' or 'why does this sentence mean that?' we have been focused on questions about what someone can *do* using a certain sentence.

In this final section, I want to connect these two strands by looking at a phenomenon sociolinguists call **social meaning**. To see what social meanings involve, consider the following pair of examples:

(53)   a. Adonis saw himself in the mirror.
        b. Adonis seen hisself in the mirror.

(Chambers 2004, 4)

These sentences express the same truth conditions – whenever one is true or false, the other will be, too, which implies that they mean the same thing, in our previous sense of 'meaning'. But there is something intuitively quite different about them. The linguist who came up with these examples, Jack Chambers, points out that nearly anyone who speaks English will recognize that 'the first [sentence] is emblematic of middle-class, educated, or relatively formal speech, while the second is emblematic of working-class, uneducated, or highly colloquial (vernacular) speech'. These emblematic associations – which involve forms of what we've previously called linguistic metadata – mean that using one or the other form will result in predictably different social effects. In many social circumstances, your ability to make friends or blend in will depend on your recognizing which one fits better where.

Very similar things can be said about the following pair:

(54) a. Nobody has heard anything about any festschrift.
      b. Ain't nobody heard nothing about no festschrift.

These examples involve a grammatical feature called 'negative concord' – dialects of English that feature negative concord are similar
to French, Ukrainian, Persian, and many other languages in marking negation at multiple sites in a sentence. Although no linguist
would be likely to say anything as crude as 'using negative concord
means you aren't educated', Penelope Eckert, a foundational figure
in sociolinguistics, observes that generally speaking negative concord
'is associated with class, and toughness perhaps, but also quite specifically with lack of education' (Eckert 2001, 122). As in the previous
example, these associations are so widely recognized that the social
results of using one or the other form are broadly predictable.

Social meaning raises a number of philosophically rich questions.
In some of its flavors, it can seem like the 'associations' between a
particular way of speaking and a particular social identity are more
like Grice's natural meaning from Chapter Three (more like tree
rings or sharks' teeth) than they are like genuine linguistic meaning. Think, for example, of the properties of a person's voice that
even over the phone allow you to form an impression of their age
and gender in just a few seconds – these seem to be properties that
speakers have little control over, and which might have more to do
with physiology than with actions the speaker might be attempting to
undertake.[2] On the other hand, it is just as clear that speakers at least
sometimes consciously and unconsciously exploit the different associations activated by examples like *himself/hisself* and *aren't any/ain't
no* to engage in identity-constructing performances like the ones we
looked at toward the end of the previous section.

Sociolinguists often point to Bill Clinton and Barack Obama as
prominent examples of how a speaker can exploit the different associations different ways of speaking have to construct a persona that fits
a certain social context. Both men held the office of president of the
United States, and both have higher degrees from very fancy universities. Obama in particular was known for a cerebral style evoking his
background as a law professor. But both were also very well known
for their ability to 'dress down' their speech, employing vernacular

expressions and pronunciations to present an unfussy sensibility and to come off as genuine while connecting with audiences.

Presidents of the United States are not the only people that modulate their verbal behavior with this kind of persona-constructing aim in mind, however. Penelope Eckert, the sociolinguist whose comments on negative concord I quoted just above, based much of her research on time she spent observing the linguistic behavior of students in schools in the San Francisco Bay Area and in suburban Detroit. One of Eckert's most famous studies had to do with patterns of speech characteristic of 'jocks' and 'burnouts' at a Detroit-area high school in the early 1980s. She found that students who participated in more school-organized activities, played sports, and expressed greater respect for authority tended to use certain vocabulary and to pronounce certain vowels in a distinctive way, and students who spent more time 'cruising', listening to counter-culture music, and experimenting with drugs and alcohol tended to use different words and distinctive pronunciations. While Eckert's labels may sound a bit old-fashioned now (which itself helps make her points!), I'd be willing to bet that anyone who remembers high school will be able to remember different cliques or subcultures and the linguistic styles that were associated with them.

Eckert's observations are particularly interesting for us here because they reveal that people – including children – do much more than simply picking up social personas like ready-made outfits off the rack. Although she found that certain sounds and words were much more common among jocks than among burnouts, and vice versa, people who identified with one or the other group varied their speech quite a bit depending on the circumstances, the topic of discussion, and the particular line they wanted to establish for themselves in a conversation. Members of one group would sometimes adopt features from the other, or play one identity up or down by making certain characteristic sounds more pronounced or using characteristic expressions more frequently.

In terms sociolinguists sometimes use, we create distinctive individual personas – both short term over the course of a single conversation and long term over the course of many – through a process called **bricolage**. Bricolage can be understood by analogy with a kind of project that at least when I was in elementary school was fairly common. The teacher would give us a stack of old magazines, scissors, and some glue and tell us to make a collage by cutting out little bits of the things we liked and pasting them together. With sociolinguistic bricolage, the things we are cutting and pasting are little bits of speech patterns, each coming with distinctive little clusters of associated properties. By combining just this pronunciation with just that bit of distinctive slang, we can create effects that are both different from the effect either would have on its own, and which allow us a much freer range of options in coming up with a style quite our own.

This process – both in terms of the mechanisms employed, and in terms of what we use it to do – raises many more philosophically interesting questions than we have space for here. Since the aim of this final chapter of the book is to look at questions concerning linguistic diversity, I'll confine my commentary to drawing out one connection with a point made in the previous section. There, we closed with the idea that different languages make different classes of persona-constituting speech acts possible, and we said that one of the tragic results of language loss is that some of those personas become unperformable. I see sociolinguistic variation – variation in pronunciation, vocabulary, grammar, and so on – as providing a similarly rich set of materials from which personas can be constructed, and I take the value of those persona-constructing possibilities to provide one reason for valuing dialectical diversity.

Earlier I said that I think a world in which language diversity makes a greater variety of possible selves performable is a richer world for all of us than a world in which there are fewer ways someone might sing a self into being. I think the very same point holds in the case of dialectical diversity – even if I myself do not make use of the full range of possible styles that variation in English makes available to me, I often have occasion to marvel at the creative ways others employ language to engage in self-construction, and even acts of types I myself never experience contribute to the vibrancy of the larger linguistic community I am a member of.

As in the previous section, one way to appreciate the significance of this richness is by looking at some cases in which circumstances mean that people can't fully take advantage of it. I closed my discussion of language loss in the previous section by calling attention to a sense in which speakers of dying languages might find themselves in the terrible situation of being unable to perform certain kinds of self constituting illocutionary actions, since no one is around to recognize what they're doing. I want to close this section by making a few related points. Suppose you move from one part of the country to another and find yourself surrounded by people who speak very differently from you. If the people there aren't familiar with your way of speaking, it might well turn out to be the case that they can't recognize the moves you're making for what they are – maybe they take you for a buffoon when you're trying to make a joke, or mistake your attempted politeness for indecision, or maybe they don't recognize some of the things you do in your speech as significant at all.

I think it's easy to see that there's a sense in which this situation has some bad consequences for you – you end up not really being able to 'be yourself' in your new environment, and indeed, less able to 'be yourself' than everyone else around you. But how philosophically significant is sort of badness? You might think the answer isn't obvious. If you come from a warm part of a country and move to a cold part, you will be less prepared than people who have always lived in the cold part to deal with the weather. You might not have the right clothes, or you might not know how to handle things like walking on slippery streets, dealing with iced-up car windows, and so on. In a case like this, you are less able than others to maneuver fully freely in your environment. That seems to make you pretty clearly worse off than other people, but not in a way that's obviously philosophically very important.

One way to argue that the limits placed on the freedom of people whose dialectical range isn't fully appreciated by their audiences are particularly problematic would be by arguing that those limits affect people in a domain that is especially important. If dialectical diversity involves the construction of a social self, as I have suggested, this strategy might seem like quite a plausible one. But I think we can appreciate a kind of badness that goes beyond this if we think about the difference between limits we face because we're unlucky and limits we face because things are unfair.

We can change the flavor of our winter migration example a bit if we think about ways in which the background circumstances of the society you live in contribute to your being less well equipped than others to move around in the way you want. Imagine that the reason you had to move from the warm part to the cold part of your country was that people from the cold part had control of the political institutions and had explicitly decided that universities should only be built in places with very long winters because they thought academic life can only properly be conducted in the cold. Or that people from the warm region who belong to certain social groups are raised with cold weather training, but other social groups are not. If the reason for your comparative immobility after your move comes down to something like this, it starts to look like we have a substantial question of justice on our hands.

In English and many (most? nearly all?) other languages, it's plausible to think that the situation with regard to dialectical diversity looks more like the unfair cold weather scenarios than it does like the unlucky one. To make this point, it will be helpful to introduce a distinction linguists sometimes draw between **productive** and **receptive** linguistic competences. As the names suggest, this distinction separates the kinds of discriminations someone is able to make when *producing* speech or signs from the ones they are equipped to make when *processing* others' speech.

We can reframe our migration scenario in these terms as a scenario in which the speaker finds themself with a range of productive competences that aren't matched by the receptive competence of their audiences – they do things in speech that the audience can't see or hear, by using patterns of speech the audience isn't familiar with. As it turns out, gaps like this, and indeed, strikingly asymmetrical ones – are extremely widespread. Speakers of **prestige dialects**, like Mainstream US English or dialects in the UK associated with 'received pronunciation' will be able to count on nearly any audience having the receptive competence necessary to track the things they do with their speech in extremely fine grain, thanks to the fact that prestige dialects are the dialects heard on TV and the radio and are the dialects that are typically held up as good examples in schools and universities.

Speakers of dialects that are less well represented in the media and in public life, on the other hand, like African-American Language and Appalachian English in the US or Multicultural London English and Estuary English in the UK, are much more likely to find themselves in situations in which their productive competence outstrips their audience's receptive competence. There will be things they would be able to do in conversation with someone familiar with the dialect, that is, that they can't do in conversation with someone who lacks that familiarity.

Since this lack of familiarity is due to unfair background circumstances – speakers of one dialect rather than the other have the power to set the standards for what news presenters, teachers, and politicians should sound like – it seems like an injustice. Since the kinds of things that speakers of non-prestige dialects are prevented from doing are arguably very important, involving nothing less than the construction of a social identity, it seems like this injustice is a serious one. In fact, this looks like the kind of thing that might plausibly fit under the definition of Kukla's discursive injustice: speech acts involving persona construction that certain people try to perform either don't come off or come off in a way different from the way intended and the way that would have obtained if the background social context had been different. This distortion is due a comparative disempowerment that affects speakers of non-prestige dialects and redounds to their further disadvantage when they find themselves less free to construct the self they want to construct than speakers of prestige dialects would be.

> Is it right to think of asymmetries in people's range of possible performances in terms of discursive injustice? What should we do about such asymmetries, if anything could be done?

NOTES

1. Maybe you don't think linguistic diversity is a good thing. You might think, 'Wait, wasn't the linguistic splintering from the story of the Tower of Babel precisely supposed to be a punishment for humanity? If we all spoke the same language, we'd be able to trade freely, avoid war, and really understand one another.' I won't attempt to argue against those claims here. Note, however, that things that are on balance bad can still have some good features. So even if you think a less linguistically diverse world would be better, all things considered, hopefully our discussion here will help you appreciate some ways in which diversity is nevertheless valuable.

2. Here it is worth pointing out, however, that both linguists and people who have undergone gender transitions have offered reasons for thinking there may be more action involved in the construction of a gendered voice than it might at first appear.

FURTHER READING

Key sources for the material presented in this chapter include:

- Ethan Nowak. "Multiculturalism, autonomy, and language preservation". In: *Ergo* 6.11 (2019), pp. 303–333.
- Ethan Nowak. "Sociolinguistic variation, speech acts, and discursive injustice". In: *The Philosophical Quarterly* (2023).

For readers who want to explore related topics in greater detail, I recommend:

- Andrea Beltrama. "Social meaning in semantics and pragmatics". In: *Language and Linguistics Compass* 14.9, 2020.
- Rosina Lippi-Green. *English with an Accent: Language, Ideology and Discrimination in the United States*. New York, NY: Routledge, 1997.
- John R. Rickford and Sharese King. "Language and linguistics on trial: hearing Rachel Jeantel (and other vernacular speakers) in the courtroom and beyond". In: *Language* 92.4 (2016), pp. 948–988.

REFERENCES

[1] Luvell Anderson and Ernest Lepore. "Slurring words". In: *Noûs* 47.1 (2013), pp. 25–48.

[2] Luvell Anderson and Ernest Lepore. "What did you call me? Slurs as prohibited words". In: *Analytic Philosophy* 54.3 (2013), pp. 350–363.

[3] G.E.M. Anscombe. *Intention*. Basil Blackwell, 1957.

[4] J.L. Austin. *How to Do Things with Words*. Harvard University Press, 1962.

[5] J.L. Austin. "Performative utterances". In: *Philosophical papers*. Ed. by J. O. Urmson and G. J. Warnock. Clarendon Press, 1979.

[6] Andrea Beltrama. "Social meaning in semantics and pragmatics". In: *Language and Linguistics Compass* 14.9, 2020.

[7] Claudia Bianchi. "Slurs and appropriation: an echoic account". In: *Journal of Pragmatics* 66 (2014), pp. 35–44.

[8] Alexander Bird. "Illocutionary silencing". In: *Pacific Philosophical Quarterly* 83 (2002), pp. 1–15.

[9] Renee Bolinger. "The pragmatics of slurs". In: *Noûs* 51.3 (2017), pp. 439–462.

[10] Elizabeth Camp. "Slurring perspectives". In: *Analytic Philosophy* 54.3 (2013), pp. 330–349.

[11] Bianca Cepollaro. "In defense of a presuppositional account of slurs". In: *Language Sciences* 52 (2015), pp. 36–45.

[12] Bianca Cepollaro and Tristan Thommen. "What's wrong with truth-conditional accounts of slurs". In: *Linguistics and Philosophy* 42 (2019), pp. 333–347.

[13] J.K. Chambers. "Studying language variation: an informal epistemology". In: *The Handbook of Language Variation and Change*. Ed. by J.K. Chambers, Peter Trudgill, and Natalie Schilling-Estes. Oxford, UK: Blackwell, 2004.

[14] Donald Davidson. "Communication and convention". In: *Synthese* 59.1 (1979), pp. 3–17.

[15] Donald Davidson. "Truth and meaning". In: *Synthese* 17 (1967), pp. 304–323.

[16] Justina Díaz-Legaspe, Robert Stainton, and Chang Liu. "Slurs and register: a case study in meaning pluralism". In: *Mind and Language* 35.2 (2020), pp. 156–182.

[17] Fred Dretske. "Misrepresentation". In: *Belief: Form, Content, and Function*. Ed. by Radu Bogdan. Oxford University Press, 1986, pp. 17–36.

[18] Penelope Eckert. *Jocks and Burnouts: Social Categories and Identity in the High School*. New York, NY: Teachers College Press, 1989.

[19] Penelope Eckert. "Style and social meaning". In: *Style and Sociolinguistic Variation*. Ed. by Penelope Eckert and John R. Rickford. New York, NY: Cambridge University Press, 2001, pp. 119–126.

[20] Gareth Evans. *The Varieties of Reference*. Clarendon Press, 1982.

[21] Gottlob Frege. "Sense and reference". In: *Philosophical Review* 3 (1948), pp. 209–230.

[22] Herbert Paul Grice. "Logic and conversation". In: *Syntax and Semantics 3: Speech Acts*. Ed. by Peter Cole and Jerry Morgan. Cambridge, MA: Academic Press, 1975, pp. 41–58.

[23] Herbert Paul Grice. "Meaning". In: *Philosophical Review* 66 (1957), pp. 377–388.

[24] Paul Grice. "Utterer's meaning and intentions". In: *Studies in the Way of Words*. Harvard University Press, 1989, pp. 86–116.

[25] Irene Heim and Angelika Kratzer. *Semantics in Generative Grammar*. Oxford, UK: Blackwell, 1998.

[26] Christopher Hom. "The semantics of racial epithets". In: *Journal of Philosophy* 105.8 (2008), pp. 416–440.

[27] Jennifer Hornsby. "Disempowered speech". In: *Philosophical Topics* 23.2 (1995), pp. 127–147.

[28] Daniel Jacobson. "Freedom of speech acts? A response to Langton". In: *Philosophy and Public Affairs* 24.1 (1995), pp. 64–78.

[29] Robin Jeshion. "Pride and prejudiced: on the appropriation of slurs". In: *Non-Derogatory Uses of Slurs*. Ed. by Cepollaro and Zeman. Grazer Philosophische Studien, 2018.

[30] Robin Jeshion. "Slurs and stereotypes". In: *Analytic Philosophy* 54.3 (2013), pp. 314–329.

[31] David Kaplan. "Afterthoughts". In: *Themes from Kaplan*. Ed. by J. Almog, J. Perry, and H. Wettstein. Oxford, UK: Oxford University Press, 1989, pp. 565–614.

[32] David Kaplan. "Demonstratives". In: *Themes from Kaplan*. Ed. by J. Almong, J. Perry, and H. Wettstein. Oxford, UK: Oxford University Press, 1977, pp. 481–563.

[33] Saul Kripke. *Naming and Necessity*. Harvard University Press, 1980.

[34] Rebecca Kukla. "Performative force, convention, and discursive injustice". In: *Hypatia* 29.2 (2014), pp. 440–457.

[35] Will Kymlicka. *Multicultural Citizenship*. Oxford University Press, 1995.

[36] Rae Langton. "Beyond belief: pragmatics in hate speech and pornography". In: *Speech and Harm: Controversies over Free Speech*. Ed. by Ishani Maitra and Mary Kate McGowan. Oxford, UK: Oxford University Press, 2012.

[37] Rae Langton. "Speech acts and unspeakable acts". In: *Philosophy and Public Affairs* 22.4 (1993), pp. 293–330.

[38] David Lewis. *Convention: A Philosophical Study*. Cambridge, MA: Harvard University Press, 1969.

[39] David Lewis. "Languages and language". In: *Minnesota Studies in the Philosophy of Science*. Ed. by Keith Gunderson. University of Minnesota Press, 1975, pp. 3–35.

[40] Rosina Lippi-Green. "Accent, standard language ideology, and discriminatory pretext in the courts". In: *Language in Society* 23.2 (1994), pp. 163–198.

[41] Rosina Lippi-Green. *English with an Accent: Language, Ideology and Discrimination in the United States*. New York, NY: Routledge, 1997.

[42] William Lycan. *Philosophy of Language: A Contemporary Introduction*. Routledge, 1999.

[43] Catherine A. MacKinnon. *Feminism Unmodified*. Harvard University Press, 1987.

[44] Ishani Maitra. "Silencing speech". In: *Canadian Journal of Philosophy* 39.2 (2009), pp. 309–338.

[45] A.P. Martinich and David Sosa, eds. *The Philosophy of Language*. Oxford University Press, 201.

[46] Mary Kate McGowan. "Conversational exercitives and the force of pornography". In: *Philosophy & Public Affairs* 31.2 (2003), pp. 155–189.

[47] Ruth Millikan. "Biosemantics". In: *Journal of Philosophy* 86.6 (1989), pp. 281–297.

[48] Ethan Nowak. "Multiculturalism, autonomy, and language preservation". In: *Ergo* 6.11 (2019), pp. 303–333.

[49] Ethan Nowak. "Sociolinguistic variation, speech acts, and discursive injustice". In: *The Philosophical Quarterly* (2023).

[50] Geoffrey Nunberg. "The social life of slurs". In: *New Work on Speech Acts*. Ed. by Daniel Fogal, Daniel Harris, and Matt Moss. Oxford University Press, 2018, pp. 239–291.

[51] Alan Patten. "Political theory and language policy". In: *Political Theory* 29.5 (2001), pp. 691–715.

[52] Alan Patten. "Protecting vulnerable languages: the public good argument". In: *Oxford Studies in Political Philosophy*. Ed. by David Sobel, Peter Vallentyne, and Stephen Wall. Oxford University Press, 2019.

[53] Alan Patten. "The justification of minority language rights". In: *The Journal of Political Philosophy* 17.1 (2009), pp. 102–128.

[54] Mihaela Popa-Wyatt and Jeremy L. Wyatt. "Slurs, roles, and power". In: *Philosophical Studies* 175 (2018), pp. 2879–2906.

[55] Hilary Putnam. "The meaning of 'meaning'". In: *Minnesota Studies in the Philosophy of Science* 7, (1975), pp. 131–193.

[56] Stepen Read. *Thinking about Logic*. Oxford University Press, 1995.

[57] John R. Rickford and Sharese King. "Language and linguistics on trial: hearing Rachel Jeantel (and other vernacular speakers) in the courtroom and beyond". In: *Language* 92.4 (2016), pp. 948–988.

[58] Bertrand Russell. *Introduction to Mathematical Philosophy*. George Allen and Unwin, 1919.

[59] Bertrand Russell. "On denoting". In: *Mind* 14.56 (1905), pp. 479–493.

[60] John Searle. *Speech Acts*. Cambridge University Press, 1969.

[61] John Searle. "What is a speech act?" In: *Philosophy in America*. Ed. by Max Black. Cornell University Press, 1965, pp. 221–239.

[62] Robert Stalnaker. "Assertion". In: *Syntax and Semantics* 9 (1978), pp. 315–332.

[63] P.F. Strawson. "On referring". In: *Mind* 59.235 (1950), pp. 320–344.

[64] Maggie Tallerman. *Understanding Syntax*. Routledge, 2020.

INDEX